PORTSMOUTH

ESTATE PUBLICATIONS
Bridewell House,
Tenterden, Kent.
TN30 6EP
Tel: 01580 764225

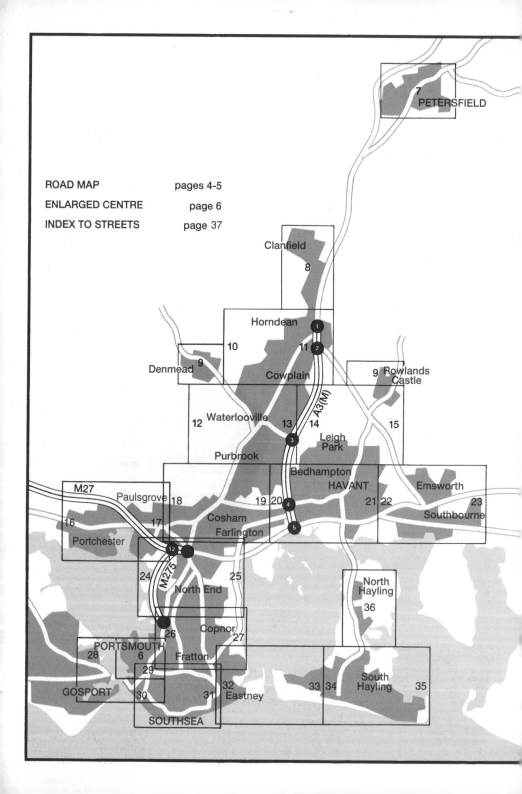

PETERSFIELD

7

Clanfield

8

Horndean

10   11

Denmead

9

Cowplain

9 Rowlands Castle

A3(M)

Waterlooville

12   13   14

Leigh Park

15

Purbrook

Bedhampton

M27

Paulsgrove   18

Cosham

HAVANT

Emsworth

16   17

19 20   21 22

23

Southbourne

Portchester

Farlington

24   25

M275

North End

North Hayling

36

26

Copnor

27

PORTSMOUTH

28   6

Fratton

GOSPORT

29

32

33 34

South Hayling

35

30   31

Eastney

SOUTHSEA

E S T A T E   P U B L I C A T I O N S

PORTSMOUTH

HAVANT · PETERSFIELD · SOUTHSEA

Car Park	P
Public Convenience	C
Place of Worship	+
One-way Street	→
Pedestrianized	▨
Post Office	●

Scale of street plans 4 inches to 1 mile
Unless otherwise stated

Street plans prepared and published by ESTATE PUBLICATIONS, Bridewell House, TENTERDEN, KENT.   The Publishers acknowledge the co-operation of the local authorities of towns represented in this atlas

Ordnance Survey® This product includes mapping data licensed from Ordnance Survey® with the permission of the Controller of Her Majesty's Stationery Office.

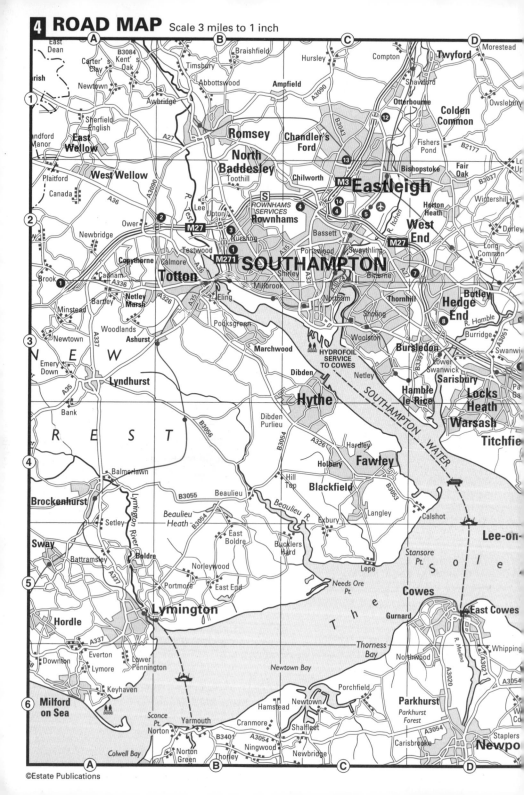

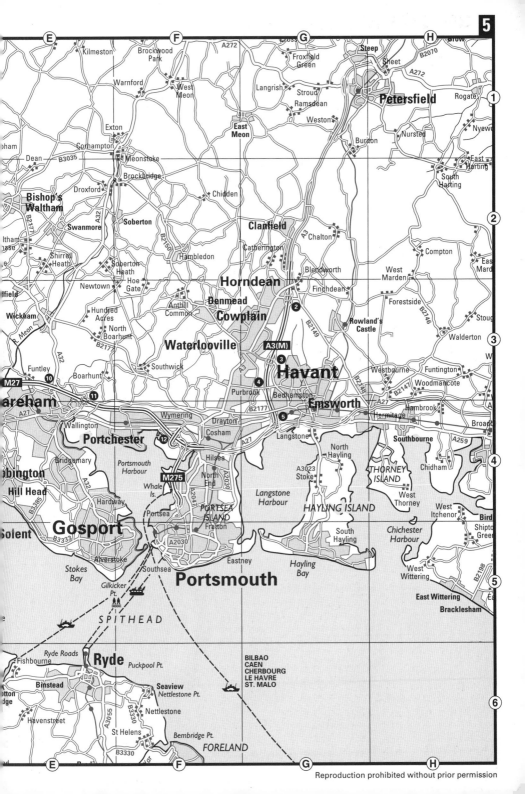

6 ENLARGED CENTRE

Scale: 6 inches to 1 m

©Estate Publications

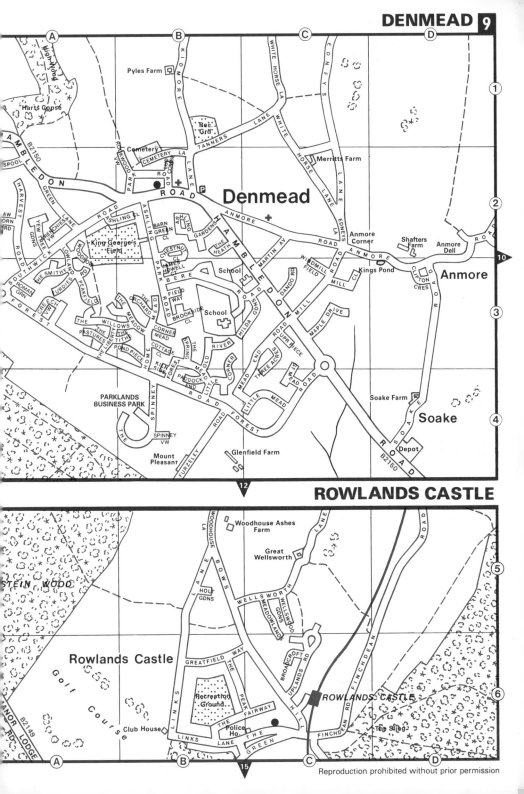

Denmead

ROWLANDS CASTLE

Rowlands Castle

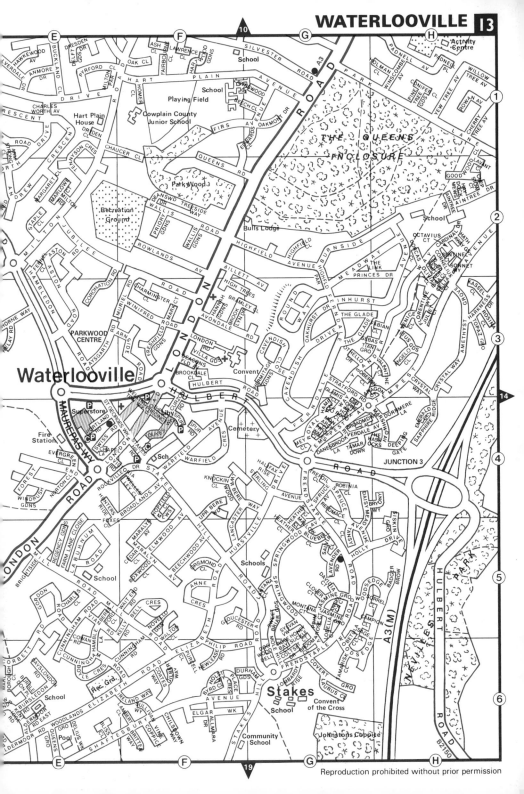

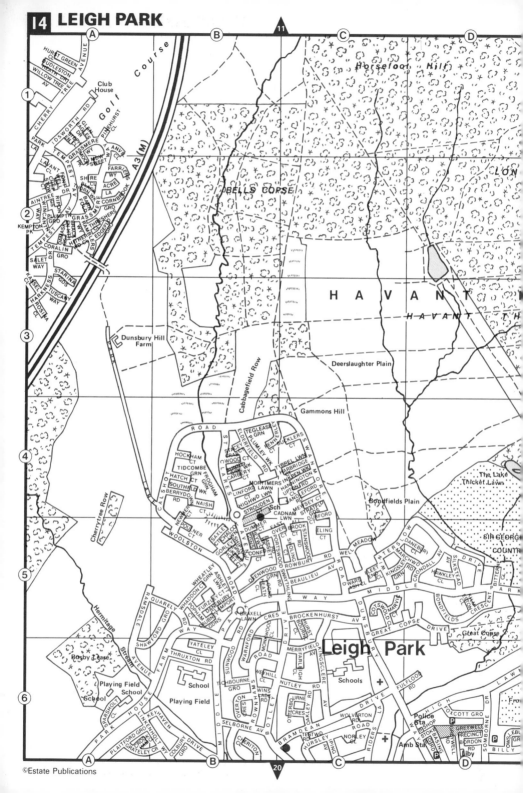

Leigh Park

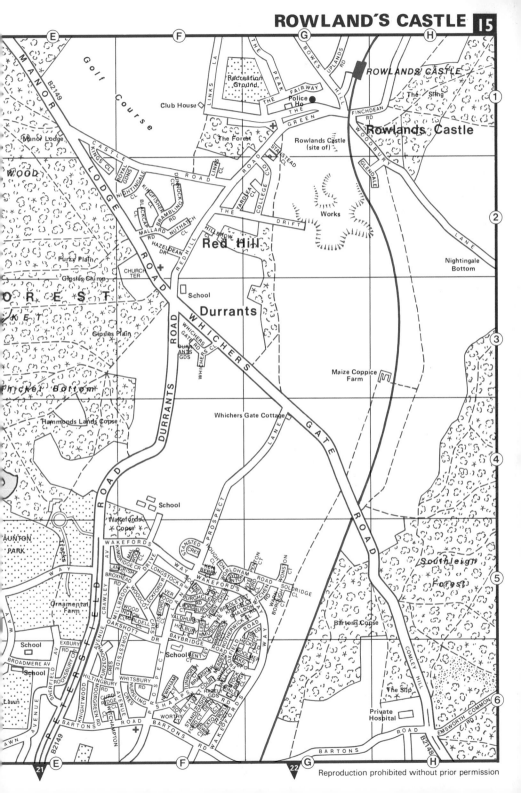

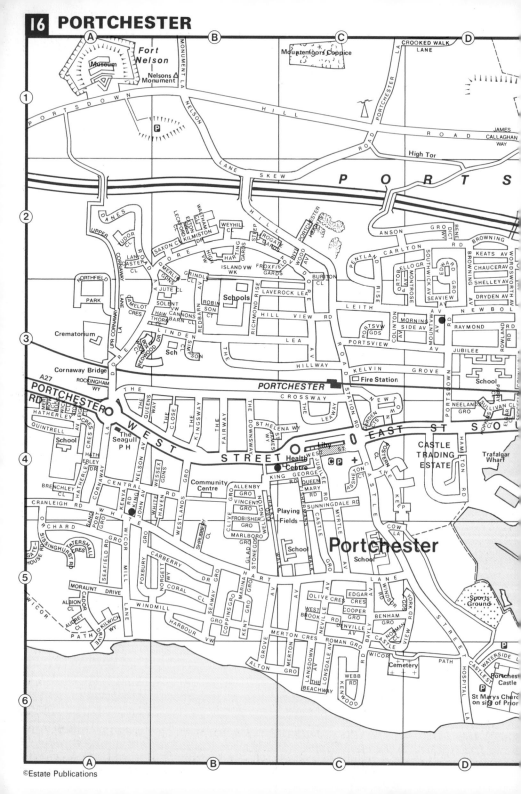

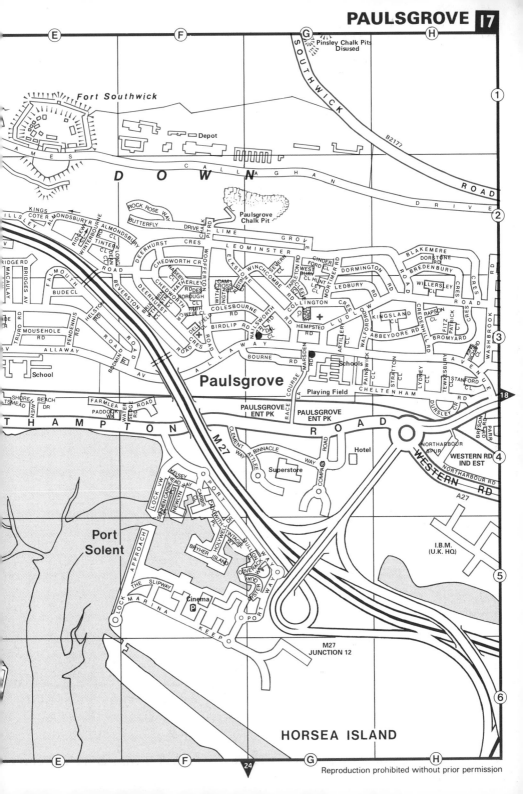

Pinsley Chalk Pits Disused

SOUTHWICK
ROAD
B2177

Fort Southwick

Depot

CALLAGHAN
DRIVE

D O W N

ROCK ROSE WAY
BUTTERFLY DRIVE
Paulsgrove
Chalk Pit
LIME GROVE
PIT RD

KINGS
COTE R
ALMONDSBURY R
ILLSLEY
RIDGEWAY
WINTERBOURNE
ALMONDSBURY
TINTERN CLOSE
CL
DEERHURST CRES
CHEDWORTH CR
WOOFFERTON
LEOMINSTER
ELKSTONE
WINCHCOMBE
CINDER
FORD CL
CL HUNT
TARLETON RD
DORMINGTON
BLAKEMERE
DORSTONE RD
BREDENBURY
CRES
WILLERSLEY
CL

BRIDGERD
MACAULAY
BUDE CL
BRIDGES AV
FALMOUTH
HELSTON
BEVERSTON
ROAD
DEERHURST
CHEDWORTH
NASEBY
WATHERLEY
RD
DESB
CAM
CROSS
KING
COLESBOURNE
WEST WAY
COLLINGTON
TARLETON RD
MORTIMER RD
LEDBURY
KINGSLAND
ROAD
RAPSON
CL
FITZ
PATRICK
CREDENHILL
BROMYARD
WASHBROOK
RD

TRURO RD
MOUSEHOLE RD
PENDENNIS RD
ROAD
ROAD
BODMIN
DELF CL
BIRDLIP RD
NAILSWORTH
RUTH WELL CL
BRYCE
HEMPSTED RD
LUDLOW
ARTILLERY
ABBEYDORE RD
WALFORD
FITZ
PATRICK
CRES
ROAD
AVENUE

ALLAWAY
CRES
BOURNE RD
MARSDEN RD
Schools
PAINSWICK
CHELTENHAM
STRATTON CL
LYDNEY
TEWKESBURY
STANFORD CL
DURSLEY

School
BOURNE RD
Playing Field

Paulsgrove

SHORE
BEACH
FARMLEA
WATER
DR
PADDOCK
SEDGE ROAD
AVEN
ALTSMEAD

T H A M P T O N
ROAD
M27
CLEMENT
ATTLEE
BINNACLE WAY
COMPA
Hotel
NORTHARBOUR SPUR
WESTERN RD IND EST

PAULSGROVE ENT PK
PAULSGROVE ENT PK

RACE COURSE

WESTERN RD
NORTHARBOUR RD
A27

KELSEY
HEAD WAY
LOCK VW
SEVEN
CARNE
NEWLYN
CABBS
PORT
DE
FALMOUTH
VINTAGE
BRYHER ISLAND

Superstore

18
4

Port Solent

APPROACH
THE SLIPWAY
LOCK MARINA
KEEP
COVERACK
QUAY
OYSTER WAY
PORT WAY
Cinema
P

I.B.M.
(U.K. HQ)

3
5

M27
JUNCTION 12

6

HORSEA ISLAND

24

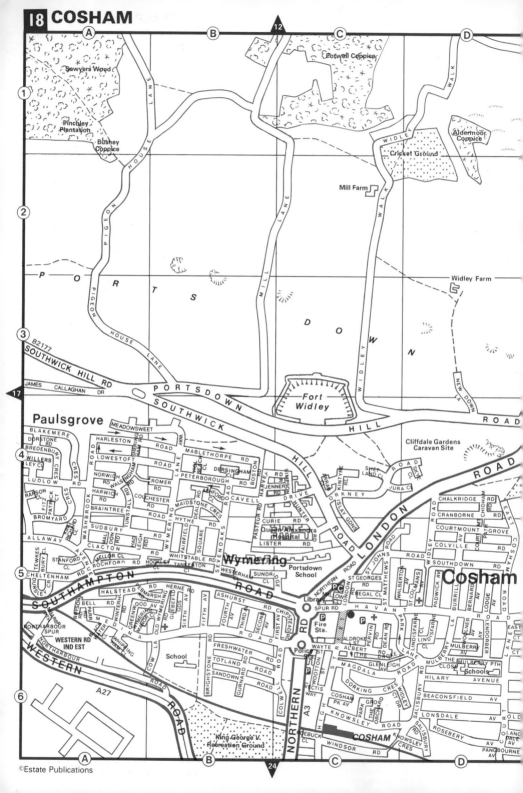

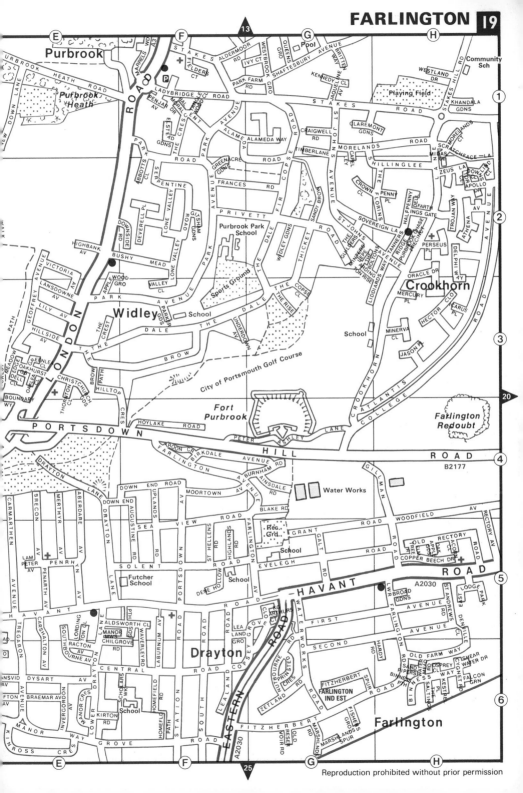

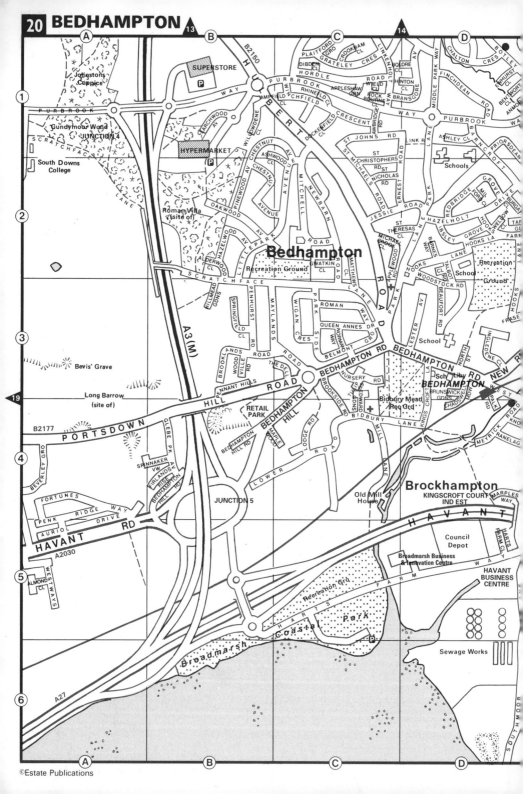

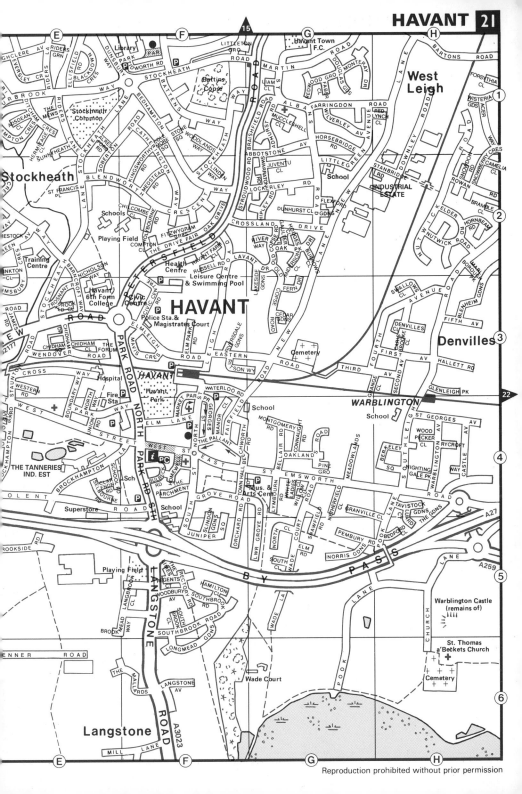

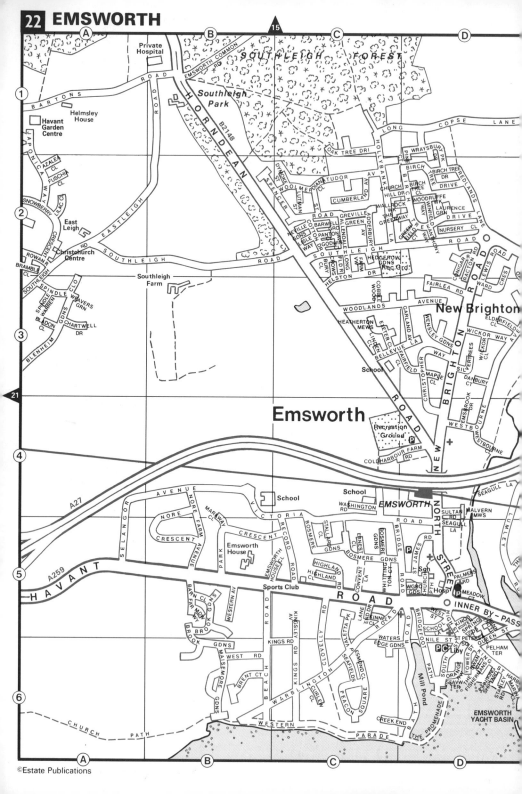

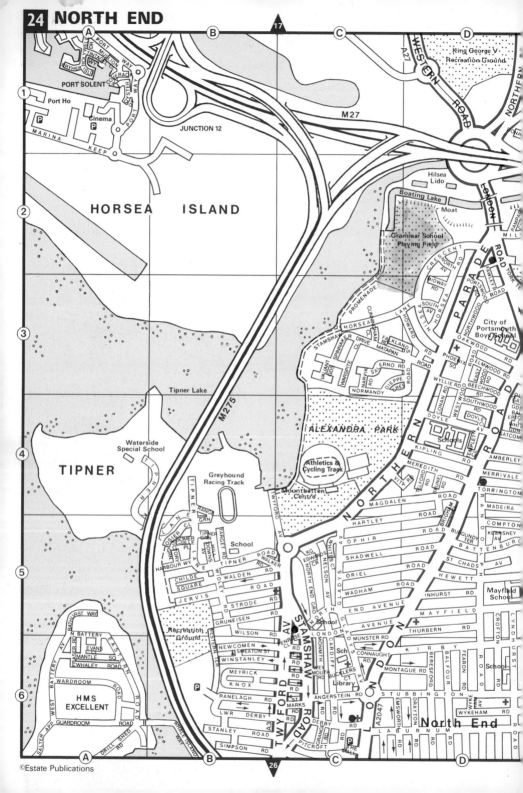

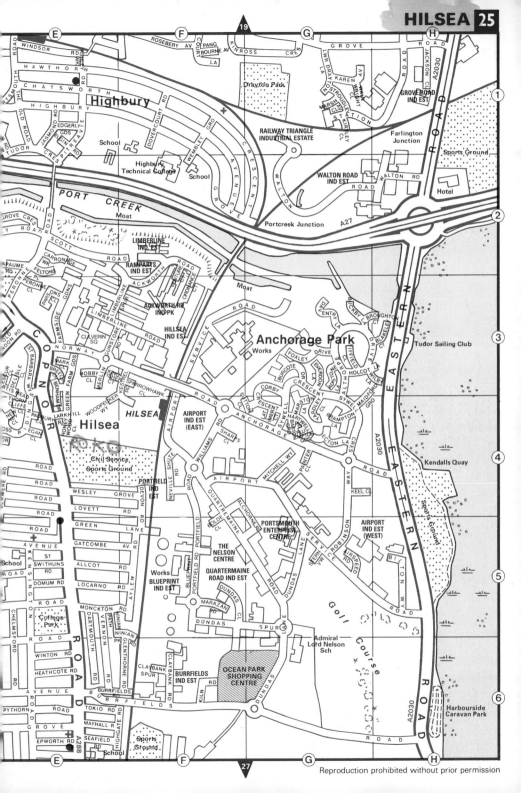

Scale: 5 inches to 1 mile

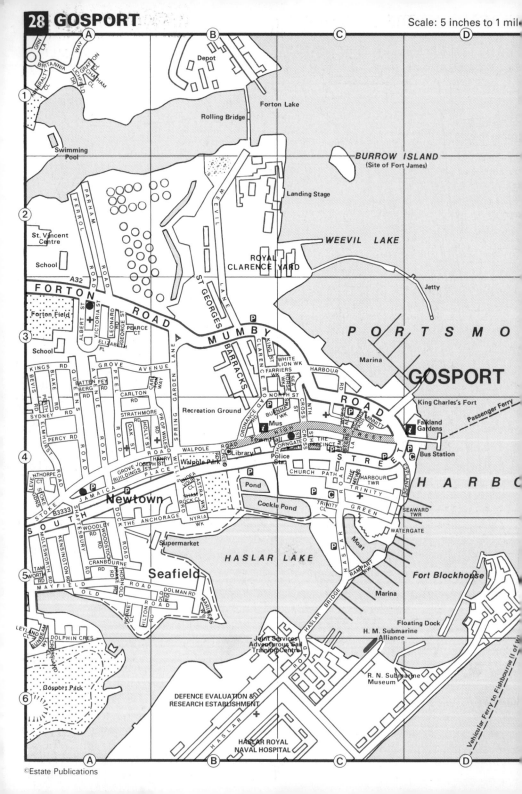

Depot

Forton Lake

Rolling Bridge

BURROW ISLAND
(Site of Fort James)

Swimming Pool

Landing Stage

St. Vincent Centre

School

WEEVIL LAKE

ROYAL CLARENCE YARD

A32

FORTON ROAD

Forton Field

School

Jetty

PORTSMO

Marina

GOSPORT

KINGS RD
BLAKE
BEVIS
PEEL
PERTH RD
SYDNEY RD
ELMHURST RD
PERCY RD

GROVE AVENUE

Recreation Ground

MUMBY
BARRACKS

King Charles's Fort

Passenger Ferry

Falkland Gardens

BATTENBERG RD

CARLTON RD

STRATHMORE RD

OAK ST
HOLLY ST

PR OF WALES RD

SPRING GARDEN LANE

ORDNANCE RD

BURNHAM WK

NORTH ST
FARRIERS
WHITE LION WK
KINGS ST

HARBOUR RD

Mus

i

Bus Station

Library

Walpole Park

GROVE JOSEPH BUILDINGS ST

HENRY ST

WALPOLE RD

Police Sta.

CHURCH PATH

HARBOUR TWR

TRINITY

HARBOR

Newtown

JAMAICA

THE ANCHORAGE

Pond

Cockle Pond

TRINITY CL

GREEN

SEAWARD TWR

WATERGATE

Supermarket

HASLAR LAKE

Moat

Seafield

RAMPART RW

Fort Blockhouse

Marina

MAYFIELD RD

OLD RD

DOLMAN RD

Floating Dock

H. M. Submarine Alliance

Gosport Park

Joint Services Adventurous Sail Training Centre

HASLAR BRIDGE

R. N. Submarine Museum

Vehicular Ferry to Fishbourne (I of W)

DEFENCE EVALUATION & RESEARCH ESTABLISHMENT

HASLAR

HASLAR ROYAL NAVAL HOSPITAL

©Estate Publications

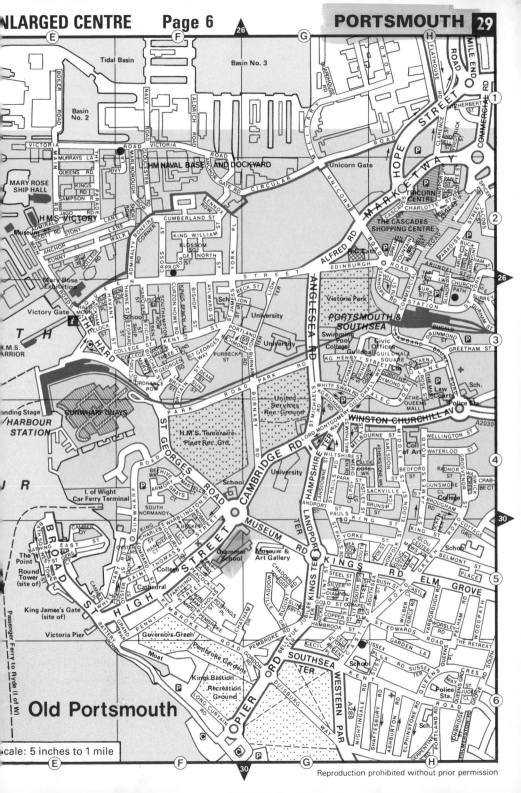

Old Portsmouth

Scale: 5 inches to 1 mile

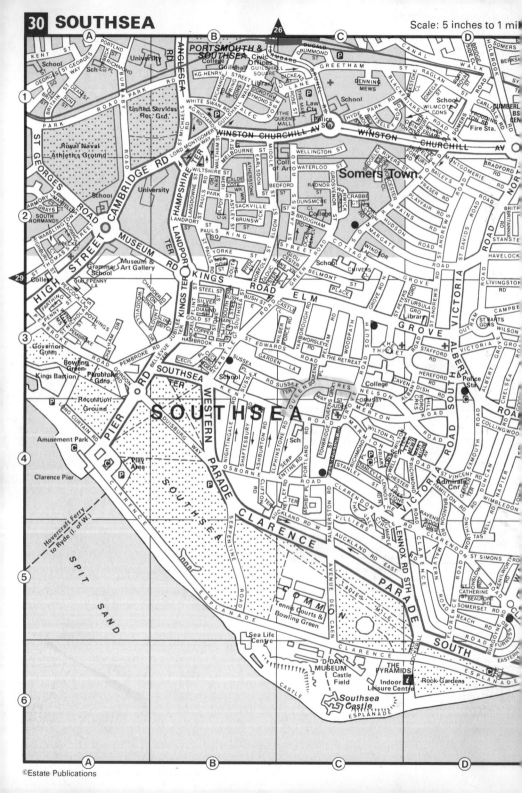

1 CHURCHILL SQ
2 FLINDERS CT
3 HOPKINS CT

©Estate Publications

Sinah Lake

The Kench

Club House

Sinah Warren Hotel

South Hayling

Sinah Common

Hayling Golf Links

Gunner Point

Club House

Miniature Golf Links

East Winner

nding Stage

Ferry

Road

Ferry Road

Links Road

Warren Cl

Sinah Lane

Sinah Park

Harbour Rd

Lime Gro

The Mallows

St Catherines Rd

St Aubins Park

North Shore Road

Sinah Lane

Lighthouse Cl

St Thomas Avenue

Avenue

St Georges Rd

St Helens Rd

Gorseway

Staunton

Seafront

Seaview Ter

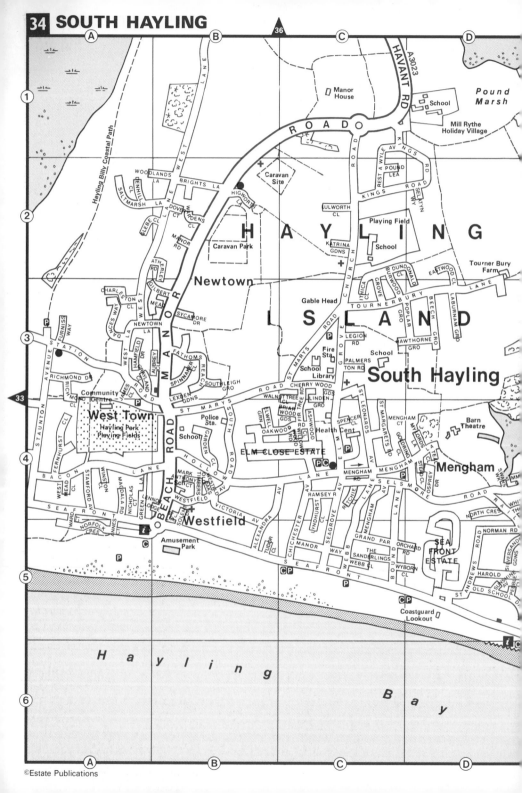

36

A3023

Pound Marsh

Manor House

School

Mill Rythe Holiday Village

R O A D O

Havant Rd

Hayling Billy Coastal Path

WOODLANDS

BRIGHTS LA

WEST LANE

SALTMARSH LANE

DENHILL CL

SLERE CL

DOVE DENS

HIGHORK CL

MANOR RD

Caravan Site

Caravan Park

ATHERLEY RD

GILBERT MEAD

CHARLESTON CL

FRANCES WAY

DANES WAY

NEWTOWN LA

WEST LANE

HAMFIELD DR

AUBREY RD

SYCAMORE DR

FATHOMS

SPINNAKER

BEACH

SOUTHLEIGH GRO

LEXDEN GDNS

Newtown

H A Y L I N G

I S L A N D

Gable Head

ULWORTH CL

KATRINA GDNS

Playing Field

School

School

KINGS ROAD

REST A WYLE AV

POUND LEA

SELSYN WAY

CHURCH ROAD

ITHICA

DUNDONALD CL

BURWOOD CL

GROVE

EASTWOOD CL

TOURNERBURY GRO

POPLAR

BEECH GRO

LABURNAM GRO

LANE

Tourner Bury Farm

TOURNERBURY

LEGION RD

Fire Sta.

School Library

PALMERSTON RD

School

HAWTHORNE GRO

GRO

South Hayling

ST MARYS ROAD

CHERRY WOOD

WALNUT TREE

LINDEN GRO

ELWELL GRN

BRIAR WOOD GDS

FIR TREE

OAKWOOD

ASHWOOD

DUNSMORE CL

SPENCER RD

ELM GRO

ST LEONARDS

ST MARGARETS RD

MENGHAM CT

MENGHAM

GOLDRING

LORDS

Barn Theatre

Community Centre

STATION AVENUE

FURNISS WAY

RICHMOND DR

RICHMOND

JAMES RD

West Town

Hayling Park Playing Fields

STAUNTON AVENUE

FERNHURST CL

BACON

WEST MEAD

STAMFORD CL

WINSHA

MAGDALA RD

NICHOLAS

ANNES

LENNOX LODGE

GREEN LA

ANTHONY CT

Police Sta.

School

GARDEN CL

HOLLOW

BEACH ROAD

ST MARYS ROAD

SOUTH ROAD

ELM CLOSE ESTATE

Health Cent

PC

MENGHAM RD

MENGHAM

OSPREY

CROSS

WARD CL

NORFOLK CRES

SEAFRONT

Amusement Park

MARK ANTHONY CT

TIMBERS

WESTFIELD

VICTORIA AV

ALEXANDRA

TUDOR

CHICHESTER CL

MANOR

LYNDHURST

SEAGROVE AV

RAMSEY R

RITCHIE

WEBB CL

GRAND PAR

ORCHARD RD

WYBORN CL

The Sanderlings

NORTH CRES

NORMAN RD

SEA FRONT ESTATE

ST ANDREWS ROAD

HAROLD

OLD SCHOOL

SILVERSAND GDNS

PEBBLE

Westfield

S E A F R O N T

WAY

CP

CP

Mengham

CP

Coastguard Lookout

H a y l i n g   **B a y**

©Estate Publications

Grid references: E, F, G, H (top and bottom); 1, 2, 3, 4, 5, 6 (right side)

Mill Rythe Holiday Village

Middle Marsh

EMSWORTH

Tourner Bury Marsh

TOURNER BURY

SALTINGS

CHANNEL

Tourner Bury Plantation

New Lords Pond

Mengham Salterns
Mengham Rythe Sailing Club

MARINE AVENUE

SALTERNS CL

SALTERNS LA

SEAVIEW

ROAD

WALK

Selsmore

BLACKTHORN DR
ILEX WK
KINGFISHER
BIRDALE
ASTRID
L SELSMORE LANE
CHANDLERS CL

North's Salterns

Lakeside Holiday Village

BLACKTHORN RD
FISHERY

Hayling Island Sailing Club
Black Point

Jetty
Yacht Harbour

FISHERMANS WK

Boating Lake
Eastoke
Camping Site

Fishery Creek

SHORELAND CT
ST HERMANS
MARSHALL RD
SOUTHWOOD
THE SLADE
CULVER DR
CAMBRIDGE DR
MEATH CL
THE STRAND
WYNDON

EASTOKE ROAD
WEST HAVE ROAD
ROBIN
BURGESS

AVENUE

CREEK

HAVEN

BIRDHAM RD

EASTOKE ROAD

HAVEN RD

BOSMERE GDNS
HASLEMERE GDNS
AVENUE

EARNLEY RD
TICHENOR RD
WITTERING ROAD
SIDLESHAM CL
PAGHAM GDNS
BRACKLESHAM RD

Lifeboat Station

WALK
SEAFARERS

Hospital

Sandy
Comm. Centre
WHEATLANDS

NUTBOURNE POINT
WHEAT LANDS CRDS
CORONATION AVENUE
TRELOAR RD

Sandy Point Nature Reserve

SOUTHWOOD ROAD
SHORELANDS CT
ROAD

SANDY BEACH ESTATE

CP

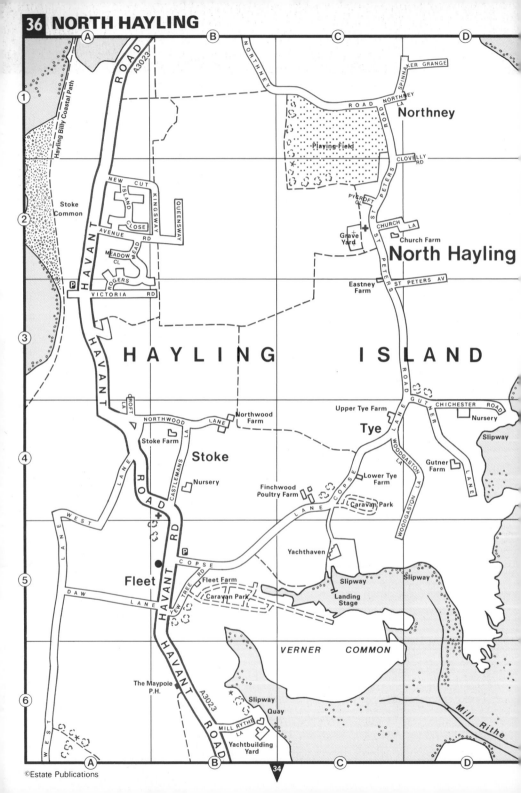

Northney

North Hayling

HAYLING ISLAND

Stoke

Fleet

Tye

Stoke Common

Playing Field

Grave Yard

Church Farm

Eastney Farm

Upper Tye Farm

CHICHESTER ROAD

Nursery

Slipway

Gutner Farm

Lower Tye Farm

Northwood Farm

Stoke Farm

Nursery

Finchwood Poultry Farm

Caravan Park

Yachthaven

Slipway

Slipway

Landing Stage

Fleet Farm

Caravan Park

VERNER COMMON

The Maypole P.H.

Slipway

Quay

Yachtbuilding Yard

Mill Rithe

Hayling Billy Coastal Path

NEW CUT

ISLAND CLOSE

KINGSWAY

QUEENSWAY

AVENUE

MEADOW MEAD

MEADOW CL

ROGERS

VICTORIA RD

HAVANT ROAD A3023

HAVANT

CROFT LA

NORTHWOOD LANE

CASTLEMANS LA

HAVANT RD

COPSE LANE

YEW TREE RD

WEST LANE

DAW LANE

WEST LANE

HAVANT ROAD A3023

MILL RYTHE LA

COPSE LANE

WOODGASTON LA

WOODGASTON LA

GUTNER LANE

ROAD

ST PETERS

ST PETERS

ST PETERS AV

CHURCH LA

CLOVELLY RD

PYCROFT CL

NORTHNEY ROAD

NORTHNEY LA

NORTHNEY ROAD

SPINNAKER GRANGE

The Index includes some names for which there is insufficient space on the maps. These names are preceded by an * and are followed by the nearest adjoining thoroughfare.

PETERSFIELD

Alderfield. GU32 7 B4
Balmoral Way. GU32 7 C2
Bannerman Rd. GU32 7 B2
Barham Rd. GU32 7 C3
Barnfield Rd. GU31 7 E3
Beckham La. GU32 7 A2
Bedford Rd. GU32 7 A3
Bell Hill. GU32 7 A1
Bell Hill Ridge. GU32 7 A1
Belvedere Pl. GU32 7 B2
Bepton Down. GU31 7 D3
Borough Gro. GU32 7 A4
Borough Rd. GU32 7 A4
Bowen La. GU31 7 C3
Bracken Rd. GU31 7 F4
Bramble Rd. GU31 7 E4
Broom Rd. GU31 7 F4
Buckingham Rd. GU32 7 A3
Buckmore Av. GU32 7 A2
Butser Walk. GU32 7 E3
Castle Gdns. GU32 7 B3
Chapel St. GU32 7 B3
Charles St. GU32 7 B3
Churchfield. GU31 7 E2
Clare Gdns. GU31 7 F3
College St. GU31 7 C3
Copse Clo. GU31 7 C3
Coxes Meadow. GU32 7 A1
Cranford Rd. GU32 7 A4
*Crawters La,
  Bowen La. GU31 7 C3
Cremorne Pl. GU32 7 C3
Crundles. GU31 7 D3
Dark Hollow. GU32 7 A2
Dragon St. GU31 7 C4
Drum Ct. GU32 7 B3
Drum La. GU32 7 B3
Drum Mead. GU32 7 B3
Dukes Clo. GU32 7 A3
Durford Rd. GU31 7 E3
Eastlake Clo. GU31 7 F3
Fairley Ct. GU31 7 C3
Farnham La. GU32 7 E1
Fern Clo. GU31 7 F4
Folly La. GU31 7 C3
Frenchmens Rd. GU32 7 B3
Geddes Way. GU31 7 F2
Gloucester Clo. GU32 7 A3
Gorse Rd. GU31 7 F4
Grange Rd. GU32 7 A4
Greathanger. GU31 7 E3
Greenhurst Way. GU31 7 F4
Hanger Way. GU31 7 E3
Harrier Way. GU31 7 F4
Harrow La. GU32 7 C1
Harting Down. GU31 7 E2
Hazlebank Clo. GU31 7 E2
Head Down. GU31 7 D3
Heath Rd. GU31 7 C3
Heath Rd E. GU31 7 E4
Heath Rd W. GU31 7 C4
Heather Rd. GU31 7 F4
Heathfield Rd. GU31 7 E3
Henwood Down. GU31 7 D3
Herne Rd. GU31 7 C3
High St. GU32 7 C3
Highfield Rd. GU32 7 B2
Highfield Ter. GU31 7 D3
Hoadlands. GU31 7 D3
Hoggarth Clo. GU31 7 D2
Holt Down. GU31 7 D3
Home Way. GU31 7 E3
Hylton Rd. GU32 7 B2

INDUSTRIAL & RETAIL:
Amey Ind Est. GU31 7 A3
Petersfield Business Pk.
  GU32 7 A3
Inmans La. GU32 7 E1
Kimbers. GU32 7 B2

King George Av. GU32 7 C3
Kings Rd. GU32 7 A3
Kingsfernsden La. GU32 7 D1
Larcombe Rd. GU32 7 A4
Lavant St. GU32 7 B3
Linnet Clo. GU31 7 F4
London Rd. GU31 7 F1
Long Rd. GU32 7 D1
Longdown. GU31 7 E3
Love La. GU31 7 D3
Lower Heyshott. GU31 7 D3
Lower Mead. GU31 7 E3
Lower Wardown. GU31 7 E3
Lyndum Clo. GU32 7 C3
Lynton Rd. GU32 7 B2
Madeline Rd. GU31 7 C2
Marden Way. GU31 7 D3
Meon Clo. GU32 7 B3
Merryfield Rd. GU31 7 E3
Mill La. GU31 7 E1
Moggs Mead. GU31 7 C3
Monks Orchard. GU32 7 C1
Montague Gdns. GU31 7 B3
*Nightingale Rd,
  Borough Rd. GU32 7 A4
Noreuil Rd. GU32 7 A4
North Rd. GU32 7 C2
Oaklands Rd. GU32 7 B2
Old Mill La. GU31 7 E1
Osborne Rd. GU32 7 C2
Osier Rd. GU32 7 A4
Paddock Way. GU32 7 A4
Park Rd. GU32 7 C3
Penns Rd. GU32 7 B2
Petersfield By-Pass.
  GU32 7 A1
Portland Clo. GU32 7 A2
Princes Rd. GU32 7 A2
Pulens Cres. GU31 7 E2
Pulens La. GU31 7 E2
Queens Rd. GU32 7 A3
Rams Walk. GU32 7 B3
Ramshill. GU31 7 D2
Readon Rd. GU32 7 D2
Regent Mews. GU32 7 B1
Reservoir La. GU32 7 B1
Rival Moor Rd. GU31 7 E4
Rookes Mews. GU31 7 F2
Rother Clo. GU31 7 F2
Rushes Farm. GU32 7 A2
Rushes Rd. GU32 7 A2
Ryefield Clo. GU31 7 F3
St Peters Rd. GU32 7 C3
Sandringham Rd. GU32 7 C2
Sandy Clo. GU31 7 F4
School La. GU32 7 D1
Selborne Clo. GU32 7 C1
Shear Hill. GU31 7 D2
Sheep St. GU32 7 B3
Sheet Link. GU32 7 D1
*Stable La,
  Folly La. GU31 7 C3
Stafford Rd. GU32 7 C2
Stanton Rd. GU32 7 B3
Station Rd. GU32 7 B3
Stonechat Clo. GU31 7 F4
Stoneham Clo. GU31 7 A2
Stoneham Pk. GU32 7 A2
Sussex Gdns. GU31 7 C4
Sussex Rd. GU31 7 C4
Swan St. GU32 7 B3
Teazle Clo. GU31 7 F4
Tegdown. DU31 7 E3
The Avenue. GU31 7 C4
The Borough. GU32 7 A3
The Causeway. GU31 7 B4
The Maltings. GU31 7 A3
The Mead. GU32 7 A4
The Mews. GU32 7 C2
The Purrocks. GU31 7 C1
The Spain. GU32 7 B3
The Square. GU32 7 B3
Thorn Clo. GU31 7 E4
Tilmore Gdns. GU31 7 B1
Tilmore Rd. GU31 7 B1
Tobys Gdns. GU31 7 D3
Tor Way. GU32 7 C3
Torberry Dri. GU31 7 E4
Town La. GU32 7 E1
Upper Heyshott. GU31 7 C3

Upper Wardown. GU31 7 E2
Vauxhall Way. GU32 7 A3
Village St. GU32 7 E1
Weston Rd. GU31 7 C4
Wetherdown. GU31 7 D3
Wheatear Dri. GU31 7 F4
White House Gdns.
  GU32 7 A1
Winchester Rd. GU32 7 A2
Windsor Rd. GU32 7 B3
Winton Rd. GU32 7 C3
Woodbury Av. GU32 7 A2
Woodlark Gdns. GU31 7 F4
Woolner Av. GU32 7 A2
York Clo. GU32 7 A3

PORTSMOUTH/ HAVANT AREA

A'Beckett Ct. PO1 6 C4
*Abbas Grn,
  Hannington Rd. PO9 14 C4
Abbeydore Rd. PO6 17 H3
Abbotstone Av. PO9 21 G1
Abbotts Clo. PO7 19 F2
Aberdare Av. PO6 19 E4
Acacia Gdns. PO8 11 F4
Acer Way. PO9 21 H1
Ackworth Rd. PO3 25 F2
Acorn Clo. PO6 19 H5
Acorn Gdns. PO8 11 F3
Acre La. PO7 14 A2
Actaeon Rd. PO1 6 B3
Adair Rd. PO4 31 H4
Adames Rd. PO1 26 D5
Adderbury Av. PO10 22 D2
Addison Rd. PO4 31 E3
Adhurst Rd. PO9 21 G1
Admirals Cnr. PO5 30 D4
Admirals Walk. PO1 6 A1
Admiralty Ct. PO12 28 A1
Admiralty Rd. PO1 6 B2
Adsdean Clo. PO9 21 E1
Adstone La. PO3 25 G3
Agincourt Rd. PO2 26 B3
Ainsdale Rd. PO6 19 G4
Aintree Rd. PO7 13 H2
Airport Service Rd.
  PO3 25 F4
Airspeed Rd. PO3 25 G5
Alameda Rd. PO7 19 F1
Alameda Way. PO7 19 G1
Albany Rd. PO5 30 D3
Albert Rd. PO5 30 D3
Albert Rd,
  Cosham. PO6 18 C6
Albert Rd,
  Southsea. PO5 30 D3
Albert St. PO12 28 A3
Albion Clo. PO16 16 A5
Albion St. PO1 26 A3
Abretia Av. PO8 10 C5
Alchorne Pl. PO3 25 F4
Aldermoor Rd. PO7 13 E6
Aldermoor Rd East.
  PO7 13 E6
Alderwood Clo. PO9 20 B2
Aldrich Rd. PO1 29 F1
Aldridge Clo. PO8 10 D3
Aldroke St. PO6 18 C6
Aldsworth Clo. PO9 19 E5
Aldsworth Gdns. PO6 19 F5
Aldsworth Path. PO6 19 F5
Aldwell St. PO5 30 D1
Alexander Clo. PO7 12 D5
Alexandra Av. PO11 34 B5
Alexandra Rd. PO1 26 B5
Alfred Rd. PO1 6 D2
Alfrey Clo. PO10 23 G6
Algiers Rd. PO3 27 F3
Alhambra Rd. PO4 31 E5
All Saints Rd. PO1 26 A4
All Saints St. PO1 26 A4
Allaway Av. PO6 18 A5
Allbrook Ct. PO9 20 C2
Allcot Rd. PO3 25 E5
Allenby Gro. PO16 16 B4

Allendale Av. PO10 22 C2
Allens Rd. PO4 31 E4
Allmara Dri. PO7 13 F6
Almond Clo,
  Havant. PO9 20 A5
Almond Clo,
  Waterlooville. PO8 11 G4
Almondsbury Clo. PO6 17 E2
Almondsbury Rd. PO6 17 E2
Alresford Rd. PO9 21 E1
Alsford Rd. PO7 12 D6
Alten Rd. PO7 12 D1
Althorpe Dri. PO3 25 G3
Alton Gro. PO16 16 B6
Alver Rd. PO1 26 C5
Alverstone Rd. PO3 27 E6
Amberley Rd,
  Clanfield. PO8 8 C3
Amberley Rd,
  Hilsea. PO2 24 D4
Amethyst Gro. PO7 13 H3
Ampfield Ct. PO9 20 C1
Amport Ct. PO9 14 B5
Amyas Ct. PO4 32 B3
Anchor Gate Rd. PO1 6 C1
Anchor La. PO1 6 A2
Anchorage Rd. PO3 25 F4
Anderson Clo. PO9 21 G2
Andover Rd. PO4 31 F4
Andrew Bell St. PO1 29 H1
Andrew Clo. PO1 27 D5
Andrew Cres. PO7 13 E2
Angelica Ct. PO7 13 G5
Angelo Clo. PO7 13 H3
Angerstein Rd. PO2 24 C6
Anglesea Rd. PO1 6 D2
Anmore Clo. PO9 20 D1
Anmore Dri. PO7 13 E1
Anmore Rd. PO7 9 C2
Anne Cres. PO7 13 F5
Annes Ct. PO11 34 A5
Anson Gro. PO16 16 C2
Anson Rd. PO3 27 E6
Anthony Way. PO10 22 D2
Anvil Clo. PO7 14 A1
Apollo Dri. PO7 19 H2
Apple Gro. PO10 23 E5
Applegate Pl. PO8 11 E3
Appleshaw Grn. PO9 20 C1
Applewood Rd. PO9 20 C2
Applewood Gro. PO7 19 E3
April Sq. PO1 26 A5
Apsley Rd. PO4 31 G1
Aragon Ct. PO7 13 E2
Ardington Rise. PO7 19 G2
Ariel Rd. PO1 26 C6
Arle Clo. PO8 8 C3
Armory La. PO1 6 B4
Armstrong Clo. PO7 13 E1
Arnaud Ct. PO2 26 B3
Arnside Rd. PO7 13 F3
Arran Clo. PO6 18 C4
Arthur St. PO2 26 C4
Artillery Clo. OP6 17 G3
Arundel Ct. PO1 6 F2
Arundel Way. PO1 6 F2
Ascot Rd. PO3 27 F4
Ash Clo. PO8 10 C6
Ash Copse. PO8 10 D3
Ashburton Rd. PO5 30 B4
Ashby Pl. PO5 30 C4
Ashby Rd. PO9 15 F6
Ashe Rd. PO9 15 F6
Ashford Clo. PO6 18 B4
Ashington Clo. PO8 11 E5
Ashlett Lawn. PO9 14 B5
Ashley Clo,
  Havant. PO9 20 D1
Ashley Clo,
  Horndean. PO8 10 D3
Ashley Wk. PO6 25 E1
Ashling Gro. PO7 9 A2
Ashling Gdns. PO7 9 B2
Ashling La. PO2 26 B2
Ashling Park Rd. PO7 9 B2
Ashurst Rd. PO6 18 B5
Ashwood Clo,
  Bedhampton. PO9 20 C2
Ashwood Clo,
  Hayling Island. PO11 34 C4

Aspen Way. PO8 11 E4
Assheton Ct. PO16 16 C4
Astley St. PO5 6 E4
Aston Rd,
  Southsea. PO4 31 G3
Aston Rd,
  Waterlooville. PO7 13 E2
Astra Walk. PO12 28 B4
Astrid Clo. PO11 35 E4
Atalanta Clo. PO4 27 H5
Athena Av. PO7 19 H2
Atherley Rd. PO11 34 B2
Atherstone Walk. PO5 6 E4
Atlantis Av. PO7 19 H3
Aubrey Clo. PO11 34 B3
Auckland Rd East. PO5 30 C5
Auckland Rd West. PO5 30 B4
Audret Clo. PO16 16 A6
Augustine Rd. PO6 19 F4
Auriol Rd. PO9 20 A5
Austin Ct. PO6 17 F3
Australia Clo. PO1 26 A5
Avenue de Caen. PO5 30 C5
Avenue Rd,
  Gosport. PO12 28 A3
Avenue Rd,
  Hayling Island. PO11 36 A2
*Avington Gdns,
  Worldham Rd. PO9 15 F5
*Avington Grn,
  Penton Ct. PO9 15 G5
Avocet Clo. PO3 27 F6
Avocet Way. PO8 11 E2
Avondale Rd,
  Portsmouth. PO1 26 D4
Avondale Rd,
  Waterlooville. PO7 13 F3
Awbridge Rd. PO9 20 C1
Aylen Rd. PO3 25 F5
Aylesbury Rd. PO2 26 D2
Aylward St. PO1 6 C2
Aysgarth Rd. PO7 13 E3
Azalea Clo. PO9 22 A2

Bacon La. PO11 34 A4
*Baddesley Gdns,
  Strouden Ct. PO9 14 B4
Badger Brow. PO7 13 H5
Baffins Rd. PO3 27 E4
Baileys Rd. PO5 30 D2
Baker St. PO1 26 B3
Balderton Clo. PO2 24 D4
Balfour Rd. PO2 26 C1
Balliol Rd. PO2 26 C3
Balmoral Dri. PO7 19 F1
*Bamford House,
  Gunners Row. PO4 32 A5
Bapaume Rd. PO3 25 E2
Barn Clo. PO10 22 B5
Barn Fold. PO7 14 A2
Barn Green Clo. PO7 9 B2
Barncroft Way. PO9 20 D1
Barnes Rd. PO1 26 C5
Barnes Way. PO9 20 D2
Barney Evans Cres.
  PO8 10 C6
Barnfield Clo. PO10 23 H4
Barton Cross. PO8 11 F2
Barton Rd. PO3 25 G4
Bartons Rd. PO9 15 E6
Barwell Gro. PO10 22 C2
Basin St. PO2 26 B2
Basing Rd. PO9 14 D6
Bassett Walk. PO9 14 B5
Bath Rd,
  Emsworth. PO10 22 D6
Bath Rd,
  Southsea. PO4 31 F3
Bath Sq. PO1 29 E5
Bathing La. PO1 29 E5
Bathurst Way. PO2 24 A5
Battenburg Av. PO2 24 D5
Battenburg Rd. PO12 28 A3
Battens Way. PO9 21 F1
Battery Row. PO1 29 E5
Baybridge Rd. PO9 15 F5
Bayly Av. PO16 16 C5
Baythorn Clo. PO2 26 A3
Beach Rd,
  Emsworth. PO10 22 B6

Beach Rd,
Hayling Island. PO11 34 B4
Beach Rd,
Southsea. PO5 30 D5
Beacon Sq. PO10 22 C6
Beaconsfield Av,
Cosham. PO6 18 D6
Beaconsfield Av,
Waterlooville. PO7 13 F3
Beatrice Rd. PO4 31 E4
Beaufort Rd,
Havant. PO9 20 D3
Beaufort Rd,
Southsea. PO5 30 D5
Beaulieu Av. PO9 14 C5
Beaulieu Rd. PO2 26 C1
Beck St. PO1 6 C2
Bedford Rd. PO9 21 H5
Bedford St. PO5 6 E4
Bedhampton Hill. PO9 20 B4
Bedhampton Hill Rd.
PO9 20 B4
Bedhampton Rd,
Havant. PO9 20 C3
Bedhampton Rd,
Portsmouth. PO2 26 D2
Bedhampton Way. PO9 21 F1
Beech Clo. PO8 13 G1
Beech Dri. PO6 17 E4
Beech Gro. PO11 34 D3
Beech Rd. PO8 8 C2
Beech Way. PO8 11 F4
Beecham Rd. PO1 26 D4
Beechwood Av. PO7 13 F5
Beechwood Rd. PO2 24 D3
Beechworth Rd. PO9 21 F4
Beehive Walk. PO1 6 B4
Belgravia Rd. PO2 26 D1
Bell Cres. PO7 13 F5
Bell Rd. PO6 18 A5
Bellair Rd. PO9 21 G4
Bellevue La. PO10 22 C3
Bellevue Ter. PO5 30 B3
Belmont Clo. PO8 8 C4
Belmont Gro. PO9 20 C3
Belmont Pl. PO5 30 C3
Belmont St. PO5 30 C2
Belmore Clo. PO1 26 C3
Bembridge Clo. PO11 35 E5
Bembridge Cres. PO4 31 E5
Bembridge Dri. PO11 35 E5
Bemisters La. PO12 28 A3
Benbow Clo. PO8 11 G2
Benbow Pl. PO1 6 B2
Benedict Way. PO16 16 D2
Beneficial St. PO1 6 B2
Benham Dri. PO3 25 F5
Benham Gro. PO16 16 C5
Bentley Clo. PO8 11 G1
Bentley Ct. PO9 15 F6
Bentworth Clo. PO9 20 D1
Bere Rd. PO7 9 B3
Beresford Clo. PO7 13 E5
Beresford Rd. PO2 26 C1
Berkeley Sq. PO9 21 H4
Berkshire Clo. PO5 30 D1
Bernard Av. PO6 18 D5
Berney Rd. PO4 32 A3
Bernina Av. PO7 12 D1
Bernina Clo. PO7 12 D1
Berrydown Rd. PO9 14 B4
Bertie Rd. PO4 32 A3
Bettesworth Rd. PO1 26 C3
Betula Clo. PO7 13 F5
Bevan Rd. PO8 10 D4
Beverley Gro. PO6 20 A4
Beverston Rd. PO6 17 F3
Bevis Rd,
Gosport. PO12 28 A3
Bevis Rd,
Portsmouth. PO2 26 B2
*Bickton Wlk,
Eastover Ct. PO9 14 B5
Bidbury La. PO9 20 C4
Billett Av. PO7 13 F2
Billing Clo. PO4 31 H4
Billy Lawn Av. PO9 14 D6
Bilton Way. PO3 25 H5
Binacle Way. PO7 17 G4
Binness Path. PO6 19 H6
Binness Way. PO6 19 H6
Binsteed Rd. PO2 26 C3
Birch Clo. PO8 10 C6
Birch Tree Clo. PO10 22 D2
Birch Tree Dri. PO10 22 D2

Birdham Rd. PO11 35 F5
Birdlip Clo. PO8 11 E3
Birdlip Rd. PO6 17 F3
Birkdale Av. PO6 19 F4
Bishop St. PO1 6 C2
Bishopstoke Rd. PO14 D6
Bitterne Clo. PO9 14 D5
Blackberry Clo. PO8 8 D3
Blackbird Clo. PO8 10 D4
Blackcap Clo. PO9 15 F2
Blackdown Cres. PO9 21 E1
Blackfriars Clo. PO5 30 D1
Blackfriars Rd. PO5 6 F3
*Blackmoor Walk,
Rotherwick Clo. PO9 15 F5
Blackthorn Dri. PO11 35 E4
Blackthorn Wk. PO7 14 A2
Blackthorn Rd. PO11 35 E4
Blackwater Clo. PO6 18 A5
Bladon Clo. PO9 22 A3
Blake Rd,
Cosham. PO6 19 G4
Blake Rd,
Gosport. PO12 28 A3
Blakeley Ct. PO3 25 H3
Blakemere Cres. PO6 18 A4
Blendworth Cres. PO9 21 E2
Blendworth La. PO8 11 H2
Blendworth Rd. PO4 31 H1
Blenheim Ct. PO4 31 G3
Blenheim Gdns. PO9 21 H3
Blenheim Rd. PO8 11 E4
Bliss Clo. PO7 13 E6
Blissford Clo. PO9 15 F5
Blossom Sq. PO1 6 C2
Blount Rd. PO1 30 B3
Bluebell Clo. PO7 13 G5
Blueprint Portfield Rd.
PO3 25 F5
Boarhunt Clo. PO1 26 B5
Bodmin Rd. PO6 17 E3
Boiler Rd. PO1 29 E1
Bolde Clo. PO3 25 F5
Boldre Clo. PO9 20 D1
Bonchurch Rd. PO4 27 F6
Bondfields Cres. PO9 14 D5
Bonfire Corner. PO1 6 B1
Bordon Rd. PO9 14 D6
Bosham Rd. PO2 27 E2
Bosmere Gdns. PO10 22 C5
Bosmere Rd. PO11 35 G5
Boston Rd. PO6 18 B4
Boston Way. PO8 11 E5
Botley Dri. PO9 14 B6
Boulton Rd. PO5 31 E4
Bound La. PO11 34 C5
Boundary Way,
Cosham. PO6 19 E3
Boundary Way,
Havant. PO9 21 E4
Bourne Clo. PO8 11 F3
Bourne Clo. PO6 17 G3
Bourne View. PO10 23 G4
Bowers Clo. PO8 11 E4
Bowes Hill. PO9 15 G1
Bowes Lyon Ct. PO8 11 F2
Bowler Av. PO3 27 E4
Bowler Ct. PO3 27 E4
Boxwood Clo,
Portchester. PO16 16 A3
Boxwood Clo,
Waterlooville. PO7 13 F5
Boyle Cres. PO7 13 E6
Bracken Heath. PO7 14 A2
Bracklesham Rd. PO11 35 G5
Bradford Rd. PO5 30 D2
Brading Av. PO4 31 G5
Bradley Ct. PO9 15 F5
Braemar Av. PO6 19 E6
Braintree Rd. PO8 18 A4
Braishfield Rd. PO9 21 G1
Bramble La. PO8 8 B1
Bramble Rd. PO4 31 E2
Brambles Clo. PO9 21 H2
Brambling Rd. PO9 15 F2
Bramdean Dri. PO9 14 C6
Bramley Clo. PO7 13 F3
Bramley Gdns. PO10 23 E5
Brampton La. PO3 25 G4
Bramshaw Ct. PO9 15 F6
Bramshott Rd. PO4 31 F2
Brandon Rd. PO5 30 D4
Bransbury Rd. PO4 32 A4
Bransgore Av. PO9 20 C1
Brasted Ct. PO4 27 G6
Braunston Clo. PO6 17 F3

Braxall Lawn. PO9 14 B5
Breach Av. PO10 23 H4
Brecon Av. PO6 19 E4
Bredenbury Cres. PO6 18 A4
Breech Clo. PO3 25 E3
Brenchley Clo. PO16 16 A4
Brent St. PO1 6 F1
Brewers St. PO1 6 F1
Brewster Clo. PO8 11 E5
Briar Clo. PO8 11 F4
Briarfield Gdns. PO8 11 F3
Briarwood Gdns. PO9 34 C4
Bridefield Clo. PO8 10 B6
Bridefield Cres. PO8 10 B6
Bridge Rd. PO10 22 C5
Bridgefoot Path. PO10 22 D5
Bridges Av. PO6 17 E2
Bridgeside Clo. PO1 26 B6
Bridget Clo. PO8 11 G2
Bridport St. PO1 6 F2
Brigham Clo. PO2 24 D5
Brighstone Rd. PO4 18 B6
Brights La. PO11 34 B2
Brightside. PO7 13 E5
Bristol Rd. PO4 31 F4
Britain St. PO1 6 C3
Britannia Rd. PO5 30 D2
Britannia Rd North.
PO5 30 D2
Britannia Way. PO12 28 A1
Britten Way. PO7 13 F6
Broad Gdns. PO6 19 H5
Broad St. PO1 29 E5
Broadcroft. PO9 9 C6
Broadlands Av. PO7 13 F4
Broadmeadows La.
PO7 13 G4
Broadmere Av. PO9 15 E6
Broadway La. PO8 10 B3
Brockenhurst Av. PO9 14 C5
Brockhampton La. PO9 21 E4
Brockhampton Rd. PO9 21 E4
Brocklands. PO9 21 E4
Brompton Rd. PO4 31 F4
Bromyard Cres. PO6 18 A5
Brook Gdns. PO10 22 B5
Brookdale Clo. PO7 13 F3
Brookfield Clo. PO9 21 E3
Brookfield Rd. PO1 26 C5
Brooklands Rd. PO9 20 B3
Brooklyn Dri. PO7 13 F3
Brookmead Way. PO9 21 E5
Brookside Clo. PO7 9 B3
Brookside Rd,
Bedhampton. PO9 20 C3
Brookside Rd,
Havant. PO9 21 E5
Broom Clo,
Southsea. PO4 32 C3
Broom Clo,
Waterlooville. PO7 13 G6
Broom Sq. PO4 32 B2
Brougham Rd. PO5 6 E4
Broughton Ct. PO3 25 G3
Brow Path. PO7 19 E3
Browning Av. PO6 16 D2
Brownlow Clo. PO1 26 A4
Broxhead Rd. PO9 15 E5
Bruce Rd. PO4 31 F5
Brunel Rd. PO2 24 D4
Brunswick Gdns. PO9 20 D3
Brunswick St. PO5 6 E4
Bryher Island. PO6 17 F5
Bryony Way. PO7 13 H4
Bryson Rd. PO6 18 A5
Buckby La. PO3 25 G3
Buckingham Grn. PO1 26 B3
Buckingham St. PO1 6 F2
Buckland Clo. PO7 10 B6
Buckland Path. PO2 26 B3
Bucklers Ct,
Leigh Pk. PO9 14 C4
Bucklers Ct,
Portsmouth. PO2 24 C6
Bude Clo. PO7 17 E3
Bulbeck Rd. PO9 21 F4
Bulls Copse La. PO8 11 E3
Bunting Gdns. PO8 10 D5
Burbridge Gro. PO4 31 G5
Burcote Dri. PO3 25 G3
Burdale Rd. PO11 35 F4
Burgate Clo. PO9 20 D2
Burgess Rd. PO9 21 F5
Burghclere Rd. PO9 15 F5
Burgoyne Rd. PO5 30 D6
Burgundy Ter. PO2 24 D5

Buriton Clo. PO16 16 C2
Buriton St. PO1 6 F2
Burleigh Rd. PO1 26 D3
Burley Clo. PO9 15 F5
Burlington Rd. PO2 26 C1
Burnaby Rd. PO1 6 C3
Burnham Rd. PO6 19 G4
Burnhams Walk. PO12 28 C4
Burnside. PO7 13 G2
Burrfields Rd. PO3 25 E6
Burrill Av. PO6 18 D5
Burrows Clo. PO9 21 G2
Bursledon Pl. PO7 13 E6
Bursledon Rd. PO7 13 E6
Burwood Gro. PO11 34 C2
Bush St E. PO5 30 B3
Bush St W. PO5 30 B3
Bushy Mead. PO7 19 E2
Butcher St. PO1 6 B3
Butser Ct. PO8 8 C4
Butterfly Dri. PO6 17 F2
Byerley Clo. PO10 23 E1
Byerley Rd. PO1 26 D6
Byrd Clo. PO7 13 F6
Byron Clo. PO2 26 D2

Cadnam Lawn. PO9 14 B4
Cadnam Rd. PO4 32 A4
Cadgwith Pl. PO6 17 F5
Cador Dri. PO16 16 A5
Cairo Ter. PO2 26 B3
Caldecote Walk. PO5 6 E4
Calshot Rd. PO9 14 B4
Camber Pl. PO1 29 E5
Camber Quay. PO1 6 A4
Cambridge Rd. PO1 6 C4
Camcross Clo. PO6 17 F3
Camelia Clo. PO9 21 H2
Camelot Cres. PO16 16 A3
Campbell Cres. PO7 12 D6
Campbell Rd. PO5 30 D3
Campion Clo. PO7 13 G5
Canal Walk. PO1 26 A6
Cannock Lawn. PO5 6 F4
Cannons Barn Clo.
PO16 16 B3
Canterbury Rd. PO4 31 F3
Capel Ley. PO7 19 G1
*Captains Row,
White Hart Rd. PO1 29 E5
Carbery Cl. PO9 14 B4
Carberry Dri. PO16 16 B5
Carbis Clo. PO6 17 F4
Cardiff Rd. PO2 24 C6
Cardinal Dri. PO9 15 E6
Carisbrooke Clo. PO9 21 H3
Carisbrooke Rd. PO4 31 G1
Carlisle Rd. PO5 30 D1
Carlton Rd,
Gosport. PO12 28 A3
Carlton Rd,
Portchester. PO16 16 C2
Carlton Way. PO12 28 B3
Carmarthen Av. PO6 19 E4
Carnarvon Rd. PO2 26 D2
Carne Pl. PO6 17 F4
Carpenter Clo. PO4 31 H3
Carronade Walk. PO3 25 F2
Carshalton Av. PO6 19 E5
Cascades App. PO1 6 E1
Castle Av. PO9 21 H4
Castle Clo. PO5 30 C3
Castle Esplanade. PO5 30 C6
Castle Gro. PO16 16 C4
Castle Rd,
Rowlands Castle. PO9 15 E1
Castle Rd,
Southsea. PO5 30 B3
Castle St. PO16 16 C4
Castle View Rd. PO16 16 C5
Castlemans La. PO11 36 B4
Catherington La. PO8 11 E1
Catherington Way.
PO9 21 F1
Catisfield Rd. PO4 31 H1
Causeway Farm. PO8 11 F3
Cavell Dri. PO6 18 B4
Cavendish Clo. PO7 13 G3
Cavendish Dri. PO7 13 G3
Cavendish Rd. PO5 30 C3
Cecil Gro. PO5 30 B3
Cecil Pl. PO5 30 B3
Cedar Clo. PO7 13 F5
Cedar Cres. PO8 11 F4
Cedar Gdns. PO9 21 G3

Cedar Gro. PO3 27 F4
Celandine Av. PO8 11 F5
Celia Clo. PO7 13 H3
Cemetery La,
Denmead. PO7 9 B2
Cemetery La,
Waterlooville. PO10 23 F2
Centaur St. PO2 26 A2
Central Rd,
Cosham. PO6 19 E6
Central Rd,
Portchester. PO16 16 A4
Central St. PO1 6 D2
Centurion Gate. PO4 32 B4
Chadderton Gdns. PO1 30 A3
Chadswell Meadow.
PO9 20 D4
Chaffinch Grn. PO8 10 D4
Chalcot Lawn. PO9 14 B5
Chalk Hill Rd. PO8 11 G1
Chalk Pit Rd. PO9 17 F2
Chalk Ridge. PO8 8 C4
Chalkridge Rd. PO6 18 D4
Chalky Wk. PO16 16 B4
Chalton Cres. PO9 20 D1
Chalton La. PO8 8 B1
Chandlers Clo. PO11 35 E5
Chantry Rd. PO8 11 F1
Chapel La. PO7 13 E4
Chapel St,
Portsmouth. PO2 26 B3
Chapel St,
Southsea. PO5 30 B3
Chaplains Av. PO8 10 B5
Chaplains Clo. PO8 10 B5
*Charlcot Lawn,
Saxley Cl. PO9 14 B5
Charles Clo. PO7 13 E5
Charles Dickens St. PO1 6 E3
Charles St. PO1 26 B5
Charleston Clo. PO11 34 A3
Charlesworth Av. PO7 13 E1
Charlesworth Dri. PO7 12 D2
Charlesworth Gdns.
PO7 13 E2
Charlotte St. PO1 6 E1
Charminster Ct. PO7 13 F3
Chartwell Dri. PO9 22 A3
Chasewater Av. PO3 27 E3
Chatburn Av. PO8 10 D6
Chatham Clo. PO12 28 A1
Chatham Dri. PO1 30 A3
Chatsworth Av. PO6 25 F1
Chaucer Av. PO6 16 D2
Chaucer Clo. PO7 13 E1
Chedworth Cres. PO6 17 F2
Chelmsford Rd. PO2 25 E5
Chelsea Rd. PO5 30 D3
Cheltenham Rd. PO6 18 A5
Chepstow Ct. PO7 13 H2
Cheriton Clo,
Havant. PO9 14 B6
Cheriton Clo,
Horndean. PO8 11 E2
Cherry Tree Av. PO8 11 F6
Cherry Wood Gdns.
PO11 34 C3
Chervil Clo. PO8 8 C6
Cheshire Way. PO10 23 H4
Cheslyn Rd. PO3 27 F5
Chester Pl. PO5 30 C4
Chesterfield Rd. PO3 27 E5
Chesterton Gdns. PO8 10 C5
Chestnut Av,
Bedhampton. PO9 20 B2
Chestnut Av,
Cowplain. PO8 11 F4
Chestnut Av,
Southsea. PO5 30 D4
Chestnut Clo. PO7 9 B2
Chetwynd Rd. PO4 31 E3
Chevening Ct. PO4 27 G6
Chewter Clo. PO5 30 D5
Chichester Av. PO11 34 C5
Chichester Rd,
Portsmouth. PO2 26 B2
Chichester Rd,
Hayling Island. PO11 36 D4
Chidham Clo. PO9 21 E3
Chidham Dri. PO9 21 E3
Chidham Rd. PO6 18 D4
Chidham Sq. PO9 21 E3
Chilbourne Ct. PO9 15 F5
Chilcombe Clo. PO9 21 F2
Chilcote Rd. PO3 27 F4
Childe Sq. PO2 24 B5

Chilgrove Rd. PO6 19 E5
Chilsdown Way. PO7 13 F6
Chilworth Gdns. PO8 8 C3
Chipstead Rd. PO6 18 C5
Chitty Rd. PO4 31 G4
Chivers Clo. PO5 30 C2
Christchurch Gdns. PO7 19 E3
Christopher Way. PO10 22 D3
Church Clo. PO8 8 B1
Church La, Havant. PO9 21 H5
Church La, Hayling Island. PO11 36 C2
Church Path, Emsworth. PO10 22 A6
Church Path, Emsworth. PO10 22 D5
Church Path, Gosport. PO12 28 C4
Church Path, Horndean. PO8 11 H3
Church Rd, Hayling Island. PO11 34 C3
Church Rd, Landport. PO1 26 B5
Church Rd, Portsmouth. PO1 26 B5
Church Rd, Southbourne. PO10 23 H6
Church Rd, Westbourne. PO10 23 E2
Church St. PO1 26 A4
Church Ter. PO9 15 F2
Church Vw. Southsea. PO4 31 H1
Church Vw, Westbourne. PO10 23 E2
Churcher Rd. PO10 23 F1
Churchill Ct. PO8 11 E3
Churchill Dri. PO10 22 C2
Churchill Sq. PO4 32 A5
Cinderford Clo. PO6 17 G2
Circular Rd. PO1 6 D1
Civic Centre Rd. PO9 21 F3
Clacton Rd. PO6 18 A5
Claire Gdns. PO8 8 C5
Claremont Gdns. PO7 19 G1
Claremont Rd. PO1 26 C6
Clarence Esplanade. PO5 30 A4
Clarence Par. PO5 30 B4
Clarence Rd, Gosport. PO12 28 B3
Clarence Rd, Southsea. PO5 30 D5
Clarence St. PO1 29 H1
Clarendon Pl, Portsmouth. PO1 26 B4
Clarendon Pl, Portsmouth. PO1 6 F2
Clarendon Rd, Havant. PO9 21 E4
Clarendon Rd, Southsea. PO5 30 C4
Clarendon St. PO1 26 B4
Clarkes Rd. PO1 26 D5
Claxton St. PO1 26 B6
Claybank Rd. PO3 25 F6
Claybank Spur. PO3 25 F6
Claydon Av. PO4 31 G1
Cleeve Clo. PO6 17 G3
Clegg Rd. PO4 31 G3
Clement Atlee Way. PO6 17 F4
Cleveland Rd. PO5 31 E2
Clifton Cres. PO7 9 D3
Clifton Rd. PO5 30 B4
Clifton St. PO1 26 C5
Clifton Ter. PO5 30 B4
Clinton Rd. PO7 12 D1
Clive Gro. PO16 16 B5
Clive Rd. PO1 26 C5
Clock St. PO1 6 B2
*Clock Tower, Royal Gate. OP4 31 H4
Clocktower Dri. PO4 31 H4
Closewood Rd. PO7 12 B2
Clovelly Rd, Emsworth. PO10 22 C6
Clovelly Rd, Hayling Island. PO11 36 C2
Clovelly Rd, Southbourne. PO10 23 G5
Clovelly Rd, Southsea. PO4 31 G2

Clover Ct. PO7 13 G5
Clydebank Rd. PO2 26 B2
Coates Way. PO7 13 F6
Cobblewood. PO10 22 C3
Cobden Av. PO3 27 E2
Coburg St. PO1 26 B5
Cockleshell Gdns. PO4 32 A4
Colbury Gro. PO9 14 B6
Colchester Rd. PO8 18 B4
Coldharbour Farm Rd. PO10 22 D4
Coldhill La. PO8 10 C2
*Coldon Grn, Heckfield Clo. PO9 15 F5
Colebrook La. PO3 27 F3
Colemore Sq. PO9 21 F1
Coleridge Gdns. PO8 10 D5
Coleridge Rd. PO6 16 D2
Colesbourne Rd. PO8 17 F3
Colinton Av. PO16 16 C3
College Clo. PO9 15 G2
College La. PO1 6 B3
College Rd, Portsmouth. PO1 6 B2
College Rd, Waterlooville. PO7 19 G4
College St. PO1 6 B3
Collington Cres. PO6 17 G3
Collingwood Rd. PO5 30 D4
Collins Rd. PO4 31 G4
Collis Rd. PO3 27 E2
Coltsfoot Dri. PO7 13 G6
Coltsmead. PO6 17 E4
Colville Rd. PO6 18 D5
Colwell Rd. PO6 18 C6
Comfrey Clo. PO7 8 C6
Comley Hill. PO9 15 H6
Commercial Pl. PO1 6 F1
Commercial Rd. PO1 6 E2
Common St. PO1 26 B5
Commonside. PO10 23 E1
Compass Rd. PO6 17 G4
Compton Clo. PO9 21 F2
Compton Rd. PO2 24 D5
Conan Rd. PO2 24 D4
Conford Ct. PO9 14 B5
Conifer Clo. PO8 13 H1
Conigar Rd. PO10 22 D2
Coniston Av. PO3 27 E2
Connaught La. PO6 16 D3
Connaught Rd, Havant. PO9 21 G4
Connaught Rd, Portsmouth. PO2 24 C6
Convent La. PO10 22 C5
Cooks La. PO10 23 H5
Coombs Clo. PO8 8 C6
Cooper Gro. PO16 16 C5
Cooper Rd. PO3 27 G3
Copnor Rd. PO3 27 E1
Copper Beech Dri. PO9 19 H5
Copper St. PO5 30 B3
Coppins Gro. PO16 16 B5
Copse Clo. PO7 19 G3
Copse La. PO11 36 B5
Copsey Clo. PO6 19 G5
Copsey Gro. PO6 19 F6
Copythorn Rd. PO2 25 E6
Coral Clo. PO16 16 B5
Coralin Gro. PO7 14 A2
Corbett Rd. PO7 12 E6
Corby Cres. PO3 25 G3
Corhampton Cres. PO9 21 F1
Cornaway La. PO16 16 A4
Cornbrook Gro. PO7 14 A2
Cornelius Dri. PO7 13 H2
Corner Mead. PO7 9 B3
Cornmill. PO1 6 F1
Cornwall Rd. PO1 26 C6
Cornwallis Cres. PO1 26 A4
Coronation Rd, Hayling Island. PO11 35 G6
Coronation Rd, Waterlooville. PO7 13 E3
Cosham Park Av. PO6 18 C6
Cotswold Clo. PO6 14 C5
Cottage Clo. PO7 9 B3
Cottage Gro. PO5 6 F4
Cottage Vw. PO1 26 B6
Cotton Dri. PO10 22 C2
Cotwell Av. PO8 11 F5
Court Clo. PO6 18 D6
Court La. PO6 18 D6
Court Mead. PO6 18 D5
Courtland Ter. PO8 11 E5

Courtmount Gro. PO6 18 D5
Courtmount Path. PO6 18 D5
Cousins Clo. PO4 31 G5
Coverack Way. PO6 17 G5
Covert Gro. PO7 13 G6
Covington Rd. PO10 23 E1
Cow La, Cosham. PO6 18 B6
Cow La, Portchester. PO16 16 C5
Cowan Rd. PO7 13 E5
Cowper Rd. PO1 26 C4
Crabbe Ct. PO5 6 F4
Crabwood Ct. PO9 14 B4
Craigwell Rd. PO7 19 G1
Cranborne Rd. PO6 18 D4
Cranbourne Rd. PO12 28 A5
Cranswater Av. PO4 31 E5
Cranswater Gate. PO4 31 E5
Cranswater Gdns. PO4 31 F5
Cranswater Park. PO4 31 F5
Cranleigh Av. PO1 26 D4
Cranleigh Rd, Portchester. PO16 16 A4
Cranleigh Rd, Portsmouth. PO1 26 D4
Crasswell St. PO1 6 F1
Crawley Av. PO9 15 E5
Credenhill Rd. PO6 17 H3
Creech Vw. PO7 9 A3
Creek End. PO10 22 C6
Creek Rd, Gosport. PO12 28 B4
Creek Rd, Hayling Island. PO11 35 F5
Cressy Rd. PO2 26 B3
Crestland Clo. PO8 11 E6
Cricket Dri. PO8 11 F6
Crinoline Gdns. PO4 31 H4
Crisspyn Clo. PO8 11 F3
Crockford Rd. PO10 23 E2
Croft La. PO11 36 A4
Croft Rd. PO2 26 B1
Crofton Clo. PO7 12 D6
Crofton Rd, Portsmouth. PO2 24 D5
Crofton Rd, Southsea. PO4 31 H1
Cromarty Av. PO4 31 H2
Crombie Clo. PO8 10 D4
Cromer Rd. PO6 18 B4
Cromwell Rd. PO4 31 H4
Crondall Av. PO9 14 B5
Crooked Walk La. PO17 16 D1
Crookham Clo. PO9 20 C1
Crookhorn La. PO7 19 G4
Cross La. PO8 11 E4
Cross St, Portsmouth. PO1 6 B2
Cross St, Southsea. PO5 6 F4
Cross Way. PO9 21 E3
Crossbill Clo. PO8 11 E2
Crossland Clo. PO12 28 A6
Crossland Dri. PO7 21 F2
Crouch La. PO8 11 E1
Crown Clo. PO7 19 G2
Crown St. PO1 26 B5
Crowsbury Clo. PO10 22 C2
Crystal Way. PO7 13 H3
Culver Dri. PO11 35 E5
Culver Rd. PO4 31 G5
Culverin Sq. PO3 25 E3
Cumberland Av. PO9 22 C2
Cumberland Rd. PO5 30 D1
Cumberland St. PO1 6 B1
Cumberland Clo. PO2 24 C3
Cunningham Rd, Horndean. PO8 11 G2
Cunningham Rd, Waterlooville. PO7 13 E6
Curdridge Clo. PO9 15 E6
Curie Rd. PO6 18 B5
Curlew Clo. PO10 22 C6
Curlew Gdns. PO8 10 D4
Curlew Path. PO4 27 G6
Curtis Mead. PO2 25 E3
Curzon Howe Rd. PO2 6 A1
Curzon Rd. PO7 13 F4
Cuthbert Rd. PO1 26 D5
Cygnet Rd. PO6 19 H6
Cypress Cres. PO8 11 E4
Cyprus Rd. PO2 26 C1

Damask Gdns. PO7 14 A2
Danbury Clo. PO10 22 D3
Dances Way. PO11 34 A3
Dando Rd. PO7 9 C3
Danebury Gro. PO9 14 D5
Danes Rd. PO16 16 A2
Danesbrook La. PO7 13 G4
Darlington Rd. PO4 31 H3
Dartmouth Rd. PO3 25 E5
Daubney Gdns. PO9 14 B5
Daulston Rd. PO1 26 D3
Daventry La. PO3 25 G3
Davidia Ct. PO7 13 G5
Daw La. PO8 10 B2
Dayslondon Rd. PO7 13 E6
Day La. PO8 10 B2
Dean Ct. PO9 15 F6
Dean Rd. PO6 18 C6
Dean St. PO1 6 C3
Deansmead Dri. PO7 13 F2
Deep Dell. PO8 11 F4
Deeping Gate. PO7 13 H4
Deerhurst Cres. PO6 17 E2
Delamere Rd. PO4 31 E3
Delft Gdns. PO8 10 C6
Delisle Clo. PO2 25 E3
Delius Walk. PO7 13 H3
Dell Clo. PO7 19 E3
Dell Ct. PO9 15 F6
Dell Piece East. PO8 11 H3
Dell Piece West. PO8 11 F3
Dellcrest Path. PO6 17 F3
Dellfied Clo. PO6 17 F3
Delphi Way. PO7 19 H2
Dene Hollow. PO6 19 F5
Denhill Clo. PO11 34 A2
Denning Mews. PO5 6 F3
Denville Av. PO16 16 C5
Denville Clo. PO6 19 H5
Denvilles Clo. PO9 21 H3
Derby Rd. PO2 24 C6
Dersingham Clo. PO6 18 B4
Derwent Clo. PO8 24 D4
Desborough Clo. PO6 17 F3
Deverell Pl. PO7 19 F2
Devon Rd. PO3 25 F4
Devonshire Av. PO4 31 F2
Devonshire Sq. PO4 31 F2
Diamond St. PO5 30 B3
Diana Clo. PO10 22 C2
Dibden Clo. PO9 20 C1
Dickens Clo. PO2 26 B3
Dieppe Cres. PO2 24 C3
Dipley Cres. PO9 21 E1
Dock Rd. PO12 28 A4
Dockenfield Clo. PO9 20 C1
Dogwood Dell. PO7 19 G4
Dolman Rd. PO12 28 B5
Dolphin Cres. PO12 28 A5
Domum Rd. PO2 25 E5
Donaldson Rd. PO6 24 D1
Dorcas Clo. PO7 13 H2
Dore Av. PO16 16 A3
Dorking Cres. PO6 18 C6
Dormington Rd. PO6 17 G2
Dormere La. PO7 13 H4
Dorothy Dymond St. PO1 6 E3
Dorrita Av. PO8 11 E5
Dorrita Clo. PO4 31 F4
Dorset Clo. PO8 11 F2
Dorstone Rd. PO6 18 A4
Douglas Gdns. PO9 21 G1
Douglas Rd. PO3 27 E4
Dove Clo. PO8 10 D4
Dover Ct. PO11 34 B2
Dover Rd. PO3 27 E3
Dovercourt Rd. PO6 25 F1
*Dowell House, Gunners Row. PO4 32 A5
Down End. PO6 18 D6
Down End Rd. PO6 19 F4
Down Farm Pl. PO8 8 C6
Down Rd, Horndean. PO8 11 G2
Downham Clo. PO8 10 D6
Downhouse Rd. PO8 8 A4
Downley Rd. PO9 21 H2
Downs Clo. PO7 19 F2
Downside Rd. PO7 19 F2
Downwood Way. PO8 8 C6
Doyle Av. PO6 24 D4
Doyle Clo. PO2 24 D4
Draycote Rd. PO6 8 C4
Drayton La. PO6 19 E4
Drayton Rd. PO2 26 C1

Dresden Dri. PO8 10 C6
Drift Rd. PO8 8 B2
Driftwood Gdns. PO4 32 B5
Drill Shed Rd. PO2 24 A6
Drummond Rd. PO1 26 B5
Dryden Av. PO6 16 D3
Dryden Clo. PO7 13 E1
Drysdale Mews. PO4 32 A5
Duddlesden Heath Dri. PO8 11 F6
Dudley Rd. PO3 27 E4
Duffield La. PO10 23 H2
Dugald Drummond St. PO1 6 E3
Duisburg Way. PO5 30 B4
Duke Cres. PO1 26 B4
Dukes Wk. PO7 13 F4
Dumbarton Clo. PO2 26 B2
Dummer Ct. PO9 14 B5
Dunbar Rd. PO4 32 A3
Duncan Rd. PO5 30 D4
Duncton Rd. PO8 8 D3
Dundas Clo. PO3 25 F5
Dundas La. PO3 25 G5
Dundas Spur. PO3 25 F5
Dundonald Clo. PO11 34 C2
Dunhurst Clo. PO9 21 G2
Dunlin Clo. PO4 27 H6
Dunn Clo. PO4 32 A4
Dunnock Clo. PO9 15 F2
Dunsbury Way. PO9 14 C5
Dunsmore Clo. PO5 6 E4
Durban Rd. PO1 26 D3
Durford Ct. PO9 14 C4
Durham Gdns. PO7 13 F6
Durham St. PO1 6 F2
Durlands Rd. PO8 11 G1
Durley Av. PO8 10 C6
Durrants Gdns. PO9 15 F3
Durrants Rd. PO9 15 F4
Dursley Cres. PO6 18 A5
Dymoke St. PO10 22 C2
Dysart Av. PO6 19 E6

Eagle Av. PO8 10 B5
Earlsdon St. PO5 6 F4
Earnley Rd. PO11 35 G5
East Cosham Rd. PO6 18 D5
East Ct, Cosham. PO6 18 D5
East Ct, Portsmouth. PO1 26 C3
East Lodge Pk. PO6 19 H5
East Meon La. PO8 8 A1
East St, Havant. PO9 21 F4
East St, Portchester. PO16 16 C4
East St, Portsmouth. PO1 29 E5
East St, Westbourne. PO10 23 E2
East Surrey St. PO1 6 F2
Eastbourne Rd. PO3 27 E2
Eastern Av. PO3 27 F5
Eastern Par. PO4 31 F5
Eastern Rd, Havant. PO9 21 F3
Eastern Rd, HMS Excellent. PO2 24 A6
Eastern Rd, Portsmouth. PO3 25 H3
Eastern Villas Rd. PO4 30 D6
Eastfield Clo. PO10 23 H4
Eastfield Rd. PO4 31 G3
Eastleigh Rd. PO9 22 A2
Eastney Esplanade. PO4 31 H5
Eastney Farm Rd. PO4 32 A4
Eastney Rd. PO4 31 H3
Eastney St. PO4 31 H4
Eastoke Av. PO11 35 F6
Eastover Ct. PO9 14 B5
Eastwood Clo. PO11 34 D2
Eastwood Rd. PO2 24 D3
Ebery Gro. PO3 27 G4
Ecton La. PO3 25 G4
Eden St. PO1 6 F1
Edenbridge Rd. PO4 27 G6
Edgar Cres. PO16 16 C5
Edgefield Gro. PO7 14 A2
Edgell Rd. PO10 23 F2
Edgerly Gdns. PO6 25 E1
Edgeware Rd. PO4 27 F6
Edinburgh Rd. PO1 6 D2
Edmund Rd. PO4 31 E3
Edneys La. PO7 9 C2

Edward Gdns. PO9 20 C4
Edward Gro. PO16 16 D2
Edwards Clo,
Paulsgrove. PO6 17 G3
Edwards Clo,
Waterlooville. PO8 13 G1
Egan Clo. PO2 25 E4
Eglantine Clo. PO8 11 F5
Eglantine Walk. PO8 11 F5
Elaine Gdns. PO8 10 D3
Elder Rd. PO9 21 H2
Elderberry Clo. PO8 8 D3
Elderberry Way. PO8 11 F5
Elderfield Clo. PO10 22 D3
Elderfield Rd. PO9 14 B4
Eldon St. PO5 6 E4
Elettra Av. PO7 12 D3
Elgar Clo. PO6 16 D4
Elgar Walk. PO7 13 F6
Elgin Rd. PO6 25 E1
Eling Ct. PO9 14 C5
Elizabeth Gdns. PO4 31 F4
Elizabeth Pl. PO12 28 A3
Elizabeth Rd. PO7 13 E6
Elkstone Rd. PO6 17 F2
Ellesmere Orchard.
PO10 23 E1
Ellisfield Rd. PO9 21 E1
Elm Clo Estate. PO11 34 B4
Elm Gro,
Hayling Island. PO11 34 C4
Elm Gro,
Southsea. PO5 30 C3
Elm La. PO9 21 F4
Elm Park Rd. PO9 21 F3
Elm Rd. PO9 21 G5
Elm St. PO5 30 B3
Elm Tree Rd. PO6 19 H5
Elmeswelle Rd. PO8 11 E3
Elmhurst Rd. PO12 28 A4
Elmleigh Rd. PO9 21 F3
Elmwood Av. PO7 13 F5
Elmwood Rd. PO2 24 D3
Elphinstone Rd. PO5 30 B4
Elstead Gdns. PO7 19 F1
Elwell Grn. PO11 34 B4
Emanuel St. PO2 26 A3
Emerald Clo. PO7 13 H4
Empshott Rd. PO4 31 F2
Emsbrook Dri. PO10 22 D4
Emsworth Common Rd.
PO10 22 B1
Emsworth House Clo.
PO10 22 B5
Emsworth Rd,
Havant. PO9 21 G4
Emsworth Rd,
Portsmouth. PO2 26 C1
Endeavour Clo. PO12 28 B4
Ennerdale Clo. PO8 8 C5
Enterprise Rd. PO8 11 G1
Eperston Rd. PO8 11 E3
Epworth Rd. PO2 26 D1
Erica Clo. PO8 11 F5
Erica Way. PO8 11 F5
Ernest Clo. PO10 22 C5
Ernest Rd,
Bedhampton. PO9 20 C2
Ernest Rd,
Portsmouth. PO1 26 C5
Escur Clo. PO2 25 E3
Esher Gro. PO7 12 D1
Eskdale Clo. PO8 8 B5
Esmond Clo. PO10 22 C6
Esplanade. PO12 28 D5
Esplanade Gdns. PO4 32 B5
Essex Rd. PO4 31 G2
Esslemont Rd. PO4 31 F3
Estella Rd. PO2 26 A3
Ethel Rd. PO1 26 C5
Eton Rd. PO5 31 E2
Euston Rd. PO4 27 F6
Evans Clo. PO2 24 A6
Evans Rd. PO4 31 G2
Evelegh Rd. PO6 19 G5
Everdon La. PO3 25 G3
Evergreen Av. PO8 10 D5
Evergreen Clo. PO7 13 E4
Eversley Cres. PO9 21 E1
Ewart Rd. PO1 26 D3
Ewhurst Clo. PO9 20 D1
Exbury Rd. PO9 15 E6
Exchange Rd. PO1 6 E3
Exeter Clo. PO10 22 C3
Exeter Rd. PO4 31 F4
Exmouth Rd. PO5 30 D4

Exton Gdns. PO16 16 B2
Exton Rd. PO9 15 F6
Faber Clo. PO7 21 G1
Fabian Clo. PO7 13 H3
Fair Oak Dri. PO9 21 F2
Fairbourne Clo. PO8 13 F1
Fairfield Clo. PO10 22 D3
Fairfield Rd. PO9 21 F4
Fairfield Sq. PO6 18 B4
Fairlea Rd. PO10 22 D3
Fairmead Walk. PO8 11 E5
Fairycross Way. PO8 11 F6
Falcon Grn. PO6 19 H6
Falcon Rd. PO8 11 E2
Falklands Rd. PO2 24 D3
Falmouth Rd. PO6 17 E3
Far Meadow Way.
PO10 22 B5
Farleigh Clo. PO9 14 C6
Farlington Av. PO6 19 F4
Farlington Rd. PO2 26 D1
Farm Lane Clo. PO7 13 E5
Farm View. PO10 22 C2
Farm View Av. PO8 8 B3
Farmhouse Way. PO8 11 E4
Farmlea Rd. PO6 17 E4
Farmside Gdns. PO3 25 E3
Farriers Walk. PO12 28 B3
Farriers Way. PO7 14 A2
Farringdon Rd. PO9 21 G1
Farthing La. PO1 30 A3
Farthings Gate. PO7 19 H2
Fathoms Reach. PO11 34 B3
Fawcett Rd. PO4 31 E3
Fawlet Ct. PO9 15 F6
Fawley Rd. PO2 24 D2
Fearon Rd. PO2 24 D6
Feltons Pl. PO3 25 E2
Fennel Clo. PO7 13 E2
Fern Dri. PO9 21 G3
Ferndale. PO7 13 G4
Fernhurst Clo. PO11 34 A4
Fernhurst Rd. PO4 31 F2
Ferrol Rd. PO12 28 A2
Ferry Rd,
Hayling Island. PO11 33 E2
Ferry Rd,
Southsea. PO4 32 B4
Festing Gro. PO4 31 F4
Festing Rd. PO4 31 F4
Fey Rd. PO12 28 A3
Field Way. PO7 9 B3
Fielders Ct. PO7 19 F1
Fieldfare Clo. PO8 8 C3
Fifth Av,
Cosham. PO6 18 B5
Fifth Av,
Havant. PO9 21 H3
Fifth St. PO1 26 D4
*Finch House,
Gunners Row. PO4 32 A5
Finch Rd. PO4 32 B4
Finchdean Rd,
Leigh Park. PO9 20 D1
Finchdean Rd,
Rowland's Castle.
PO9 15 G1
Fir Copse Rd. PO7 19 G2
Fir Tree Gdns. PO8 11 G4
Fir Tree Rd. PO11 34 C4
Firgrove Cres. PO3 25 E2
Firlands Rise. PO9 20 B4
Firs Av. PO7 13 F1
First Av, Cosham. PO6 18 C5
First Av,
Farlington. PO6 19 G5
First Av,
Havant. PO9 21 H3
First Av,
Horndean. PO8 8 C4
First Av,
Southbourne. PO10 23 G5
Fishermans Wk,
Hayling Island. PO11 35 G5
Fishermans Wk,
Portchester. PO16 16 C4
Fishers Gro. PO6 19 G6
Fishery La. PO11 35 E5
Fitzherbert Rd. PO6 19 G6
Fitzherbert Spur. PO6 19 G6
Fitzherbert St. PO1 29 H1
Fitzpatrick Ct. PO6 18 A4
Fitzroy Walk. PO1 26 B5
Fitzwygram Cres. PO8 21 F2
Five Heads Rd. PO8 11 F1

Flag Walk. PO8 10 D4
Flathouse Rd. PO1 29 H1
Fleetend Clo. PO9 14 C5
Flexford Gdns. PO9 21 G2
Flinders Ct. PO4 32 A5
Flint St. PO5 30 B3
Florence Rd. PO5 30 D5
Florentine Way. PO7 13 H3
Flying Bull Clo. PO2 26 B2
Flying Bull La. PO2 26 B2
Folkestone Rd. PO3 27 E3
Fontwell Mews. PO7 14 A2
Fontwell Rd. PO5 30 C4
Fordingbridge Rd. PO4 32 A4
Foreland Ct. PO11 35 E5
Forest Av. PO8 11 E5
Forest Clo. PO8 10 D5
Forest End. PO7 13 E4
Forest Mead. PO7 9 B4
Forest Rd. PO7 9 A3
Forestside Av. PO9 15 F5
Forsythia Clo. PO9 21 H1
Fort Cumberland Rd.
PO4 32 B4
*Fort View House,
Royal Gate. PO4 31 H4
Forton Rd,
Gosport. PO12 28 A3
Forton Rd,
Portsmouth. PO1 26 C5
Fortunes Way. PO9 20 A4
Foster Rd. PO1 26 B4
Fountain St. PO1 6 E2
*Four Marks Grn,
Wyeford Clo. PO9 15 G5
Fourth Av,
Cosham. PO6 18 B5
Fourth Av,
Havant. PO9 21 H3
Fourth St. PO1 26 D4
Foxbury Gro. PO16 16 A5
Foxbury La. PO10 23 F2
Foxcott Gro. PO9 14 D6
Foxes Clo. PO7 13 E5
Foxley Dri. PO3 25 G3
Frances Rd. PO7 19 F2
Francis Av. PO4 31 F4
Francis Rd. PO8 8 C4
Frankland Ter. PO10 22 D6
Frarydene. PO10 23 G6
Fraser Gdns. PO10 23 H4
Fraser Rd,
Havant. PO9 20 D3
Fraser Rd,
HMS Excellent. PO2 24 A6
Fraser Rd,
Southsea. PO5 30 D2
Fratton Rd. PO1 26 C4
Frederick St. PO1 29 H1
*Freefolk Grn,
Warbrook Clo. PO9 15 F5
Freestone Rd. PO5 30 C4
French St. PO1 29 F5
Frenchies View. PO9 9 A2
Frendstaple Rd. PO7 13 G6
Frensham Rd. PO4 31 F2
Freshfield Gdns. PO7 13 F3
Freshwater Rd. PO6 18 B6
Friary Clo. PO5 30 C4
*Frobisher Gdns,
School La. PO10 22 D5
Frobisher Gro. PO16 16 B4
Froddington Rd. PO5 30 D1
Frogham Grn. PO9 14 B5
Frogmore La. PO8 10 D4
Frogmore Rd. PO4 31 G1
Froxfield Gdns. PO16 16 C2
Froxfield Rd. PO9 15 F6
Froyle Ct. PO9 15 F6
Fulflood Rd. PO9 14 C6
Fullerton Clo. PO9 15 F5
Fulmer Walk. PO8 10 C4
Funtington Rd. PO2 26 D2
Furdies. PO7 9 A3
Furness Rd. PO5 30 D6
Furniss Way. PO11 34 A3
Furnston Gro. PO10 23 H4
Furze La. PO4 27 H6
Furze Way. PO8 11 F4
Furzedown Cres. PO9 15 E6
Furzeley Ct. PO9 14 B5
Furzeley Rd. PO7 9 B4
Fuschia Clo. PO9 22 A2
Fyning St. PO1 26 B5

Gains Rd. PO4 31 E4

Galaxie Rd. PO8 11 E5
Galt Rd. PO6 19 G5
Gamble Rd. PO2 26 B2
Garden Clo. PO11 34 B4
Garden Ct. PO16 16 C4
Garden La. PO5 30 B3
Garden Ter. PO5 30 D4
Garfield Rd. PO2 26 A2
Garland Av. PO10 22 D3
Garnier St. PO1 26 B6
Garsons Rd. PO10 23 G5
Gatcombe Av. PO3 25 E5
Gatcombe Dri. PO2 24 D4
*Gate House,
Royal Gate. PO4 31 H4
Gatehouse Rd. PO16 16 A5
Gaulter Clo. PO9 21 G2
Geoffrey Av. PO7 19 E3
George Byng Way.
PO1 26 A2
George St,
Gosport PO12 28 A3
George St,
Portsmouth. PO1 26 C3
Gibraltar Rd. PO4 32 B4
Gilbert Mead. PO11 34 B3
Gilbert Way. PO7 13 F6
Gillman Rd. PO6 19 H4
Gitsham Gdns. PO7 19 F2
Gladstone Gdns. PO16 16 B5
Gladstone Pl. PO2 26 B2
Gladys Av,
Cowplain. PO8 11 E5
Gladys Av,
Portsmouth. PO2 24 C5
Glamis Clo. PO7 13 G3
Glamorgan Rd. PO8 8 B5
Glasgow Rd. PO4 32 A4
Glasspool. PO7 9 A2
Glebe Clo. PO11 34 A2
Glebe Park Av. PO9 20 B4
Glebefield Gdns. PO6 18 B5
Glencoe Rd. PO1 26 D3
Glendale. PO9 15 G2
Gleneagles Dri. PO7 14 A1
Glenleigh Av. PO6 18 C6
Glenleigh Pk. PO9 21 H3
Glenthorne Rd. PO3 25 F6
Glenwood Gdns. PO8 10 D6
Glenwood Rd. PO10 23 H4
Glidden Clo. PO1 26 B6
Gloucester Mews. PO5 30 C2
Gloucester Pl. PO5 30 C3
Gloucester Rd,
Portsmouth. PO1 6 B1
Gloucester Rd,
Waterlooville. PO7 13 F5
Gloucester Ter. PO5 30 B2
Gloucester Vw. PO5 30 C2
Godiva Lawn. PO4 32 B4
Godwin Clo. PO10 22 C2
Godwin Cres. PO8 8 C3
Godwit Rd. PO4 27 G5
Gofton Av. PO6 19 E6
Gold St. PO5 30 B3
Goldcrest Clo. PO8 11 E2
Goldring Clo. PO11 34 C4
Goldsmith Av. PO4 31 E1
Goodwin Clo. PO8 13 H2
Goodwood Ct. PO10 23 H6
Goodwood Rd. PO5 30 D4
Gordon Rd,
Portsmouth. PO1 30 A3
Gordon Rd,
Southbourne. PO10 23 E6
Gordon Rd,
Waterlooville. PO7 13 E5
Goring Av. PO8 8 C3
Gorley Ct. PO9 14 B5
Gorseway. PO11 33 H4
Grafton Clo. PO12 28 A1
Grafton St. PO2 26 A3
Graham Rd. PO4 31 E3
Granada Clo. PO8 11 E5
Granada Rd. PO4 31 E5
Grand Par,
Portsmouth. PO1 29 F5
Grand Par,
Waterlooville. PO7 13 E5
Grange Clo. PO9 21 G3
Grange Rd. PO2 24 C6
Grant Rd. PO6 19 G5
Granville Clo. PO9 21 G4
Grassmere Way. PO7 14 A2
Grateley Cres. PO9 20 C1
Grayland Clo. PO11 34 A3

Grays Ct. PO1 6 C4
Grayshott Rd. PO4 31 F2
Great Copse Dri. PO9 14 C5
Great Mead. PO7 9 C4
Great Southsea St.
PO5 30 B3
Greatfield Way. PO9 9 B6
Grebe Clo,
Cowplain. PO8 10 C5
Grebe Clo,
Emsworth. PO10 23 F2
Green Farm Gdns.
PO3 25 E4
Green La. PO8 8 A1
Green La.
Clanfield. PO8 8 C3
Green La,
Denmead. PO7 9 A2
Green La,
Gosport. PO12 28 A1
Green La,
Hayling Island. PO11 34 A4
Green La,
Portsmouth. PO3 25 E5
Green Rd. PO5 6 F4
Greenacre Gdns. PO7 19 F2
Greenfield Court. PO10 22 D2
Greenfield Cres. PO8 11 F4
Greenfield Rise. PO8 11 F6
Greenlea Clo. PO7 19 E3
Greenwood Av. PO6 18 A5
Greetham St. PO5 6 F3
Grenville Rd. PO4 31 E2
Greville Grn. PO10 22 C2
Greywell Precinct. PO9 14 D6
Greywell Rd. PO9 14 D6
Grindle Clo. PO16 16 B2
Gritanwood Rd. PO4 32 A4
Grosvenor St. PO5 6 F4
Grove Av,
Gosport. PO12 28 A3
Grove Av,
Portchester. PO16 16 B6
Grove Buildings. PO12 28 A4
Grove Rd,
Cosham. PO6 19 E6
Grove Rd, Havant. PO9 21 F4
Grove Rd North. PO5 30 C3
Grove Rd South. PO5 30 C4
Gruneisen Rd. PO2 24 B5
Guardhouse Rd. PO1 29 G1
Guardroom Rd. PO24 24 A6
Guildford Clo. PO10 23 H5
Guildford Rd. PO1 26 C5
Guildhall Sq. PO1 29 H3
Guildhall Walk. PO1 6 E3
Gun Wharf Rd. PO1 6 B4
Gunners Row. PO4 31 H4
Gunstore Rd. PO3 25 E3
Gurnard Rd. PO6 18 B6
Gurney Rd. PO4 32 A3
Gutner La. PO11 36 D4
Gwatkin Clo. PO9 20 C2
Gypsy La. PO8 10 D4

Hadleigh Rd. PO6 18 A5
Hale St North. PO1 26 B4
Hale St South. PO1 26 B5
Half Moon St. PO1 6 B2
Halfpenny Dell. PO7 19 H2
Halfpenny La. PO1 30 A3
Halifax Rise. PO7 13 G4
Hallett Rd. PO9 21 H3
Halliday Cres. PO4 32 B4
*Halliday House,
Gunners Row. PO4 32 A5
Halstead Rd. PO6 18 A5
Ham La,
Horndean. PO8 11 E1
Ham La,
Southbourne. PO10 23 G6
Hamble La. PO7 13 E6
Hambledon Par. PO7 12 D1
Hambledon Rd,
Clanfield. PO8 8 A2
Hambledon Rd,
Denmead. PO7 9 A1
Hambledon Rd,
Waterlooville. PO7 13 E5
Hambrook St. PO5 30 B3
Hamfield Dri. PO11 34 A3
Hamilton Clo. PO9 21 F5
Hamilton Rd,
Portchester. PO6 16 D4
Hamilton Rd,
Southsea. PO5 30 D4

Hampshire St. PO1 26 C4
Hampshire Ter. PO1 6 D4
Hampton Clo. PO7 13 G4
Hannah Gdns. PO7 13 F3
Hannington Rd. PO9 14 C4
Hanover Clo. PO1 29 F5
Hanover St. PO1 6 B2
Hanway Rd. PO1 26 B3
Harbour Rd,
Gosport. PO12 28 C3
Harbour Rd,
Hayling Island. PO11 33 G3
Harbour Tower. PO12 28 C4
Harbour Vw. PO16 16 B5
*Harbour Walk,
Broad St. PO1 29 E5
Harbour Way,
Emsworth. PO10 22 D6
Harbour Way,
Portsmouth. PO2 24 B5
Harbridge Ct. PO9 14 C4
Harcourt Clo. PO8 11 E5
Harcourt Rd. PO1 26 C3
Hardy Rd. PO6 19 H6
Harestock Rd. PO9 21 E2
Harkness Dri. PO7 14 A3
Harleston Rd. PO6 18 A4
Harley Wik. PO1 26 B5
Harold Rd,
Hayling Island. PO11 34 D5
Harold Rd,
Southsea. PO4 31 E3
Harold Rd,
Westbourne. PO10 23 E2
Harrier Clo. PO8 11 E2
Harrow Rd. PO5 31 E2
Hart Plain Av,
Waterlooville. PO8 13 F1
Hart Plain Av,
Wecock. PO8 10 C5
Harting Clo. PO8 8 C3
Harting Gdns. PO16 16 B2
Hartland Ct. PO10 23 G5
Hartley Rd. PO2 24 C5
Harts Farm Clo. PO9 20 D5
Harts Farm Way. PO9 20 C5
Hartwell Rd. PO3 25 G4
Hartwood Gdns. PO8 13 F1
*Harvest Gate Walk,
Woolston Rd. PO9 14 B5
Harvest Rd. PO7 9 A2
*Harvey House,
Gunners Row. PO4 32 A5
Harvey Rd. PO6 18 B4
Harwich Rd. PO6 18 A4
Haslar Bri. PO12 28 B4
Haslar Cres. PO7 12 D1
Haslar Rd. PO12 28 B6
Haslemere Gdns. PO11 35 G5
Haslemere Rd,
Southbourne. PO10 23 G4
Haslemere Rd,
Southsea. PO4 31 F4
Hatch Ct. PO9 14 B4
Hatfield Rd. PO4 31 G3
Hathaway Gdns. PO7 13 H2
Hatherley Cres. PO16 16 A4
Hatherley Dri. PO16 16 A4
Hatherley Rd. PO6 17 F3
Havant By-Pass. PO9 20 D4
Havant Farm Clo. PO9 21 F2
Havant Rd,
Cosham. PO6 18 C5
Havant Rd,
Emsworth. PO10 22 A5
Havant Rd,
Hayling Island. PO11 36 A3
Havant Rd,
Horndean. PO8 11 H2
Havant Rd,
Portsmouth. PO2 26 B1
Havant St. PO1 6 B2
Havelock Rd. PO5 30 D2
Haven Rd. PO11 35 F5
Havisham Rd. PO2 26 A3
Hawke St. PO1 6 B2
Hawkewood Av. PO7 10 B6
Hawkley Clo. PO9 14 D5
*Hawstead Grn,
Mewsey Ct. PO9 14 C4
Hawthorn Clo. PO16 16 B3
Hawthorn Cres. PO6 25 E1
Hawthorn Rd,
Denmead. PO7 9 A2
Hawthorn Rd,
Horndean. PO8 8 C5

Hawthorne Gro. PO11 34 D3
Hay St. PO1 6 C2
Haydock Mews. PO7 13 H2
Hayling Av. PO3 27 E4
Haywards Ct. PO1 6 B4
Hazel Gro. PO8 8 C2
Hazel Rd. PO8 8 C2
Hazeldean Dri. PO9 15 F2
Hazelholt Dri. PO9 20 D2
Hazelwood Av. PO9 20 B2
Hazely Gdns. PO9 15 F6
Hazleton Way. PO8 11 F3
Heath Clo. PO8 11 F2
Heathcote Rd. PO2 25 E6
Heather Clo. PO7 13 G5
Heatherton Mws. PO10 22 C3
Heathfield Rd. PO2 26 B2
Hector Clo. PO7 19 H3
*Hedge End Walk,
Soldridge Clo. PO9 15 G5
Hedgerow Gdns. PO10 22 C2
Heidelberg Rd. PO4 31 F2
Helena Rd. PO4 31 F5
Hellyer Rd. PO4 31 G4
Helston Dri. PO10 22 C3
Helston Rd. PO6 17 E3
Hemlock Rd. PO8 10 C5
Hempsted Rd. PO6 17 G3
Hemsley Walk. PO8 11 E5
Henderson Rd. PO4 32 A4
Henley Rd. PO4 31 F4
Herbert Rd. PO4 31 E4
Herbert St. PO1 26 A3
Hercules St. PO2 26 B2
Hereford Rd. PO5 30 D3
Hermitage Clo. PO9 21 E1
Hermitage Gdns. PO7 13 G3
Herne Rd. PO6 18 B5
Heron Clo. PO4 27 F6
Heron Quay. PO10 23 E6
Herriot Clo. PO8 11 E4
Hertford Pl. PO1 26 B4
Hester Rd. PO4 32 A3
Hewett Rd. PO2 24 D5
Heyshott Gdns. PO8 8 C3
Heyshott Rd. PO4 31 F2
Heyward Rd. PO4 31 E2
Heywood Gdns. PO9 14 B5
High Lawn Way. PO9 14 D6
High St,
Cosham. PO6 18 C6
High St,
Emsworth. PO10 22 D5
High St,
Gosport. PO12 28 C4
High St,
Portsmouth. PO1 29 E5
High Trees. PO7 13 F3
High View. PO16 16 B2
Highbank Av. PO7 19 E2
Highbury Gro. PO6 25 E1
Highbury St. PO1 30 A2
Highbury Way. PO6 25 E1
Highclere Av. PO9 21 E1
Highcroft La. PO8 11 G1
Highfield Av. PO7 13 F2
Highfield Clo. PO7 13 G2
Highfield Par. PO7 13 G2
Highfield Rd. PO1 26 B6
Highgate Rd. PO3 25 E6
Highgrove Rd. PO3 27 F3
Highland Clo. PO10 22 C5
Highland Rd,
Emsworth. PO10 22 C5
Highland Rd,
Southsea. PO4 31 F4
Highland St. PO4 31 G4
Highland Ter. PO4 31 F4
Highlands Rd. PO6 19 F5
Highwood Lawn. PO9 14 B4
Higworth La. PO11 34 B2
Hilary Av. PO6 18 D6
Hilda Gdns. PO7 9 C3
Hill Downs Av. PO2 24 B5
Hill Rd. PO16 16 B2
Hill View Rd. PO16 16 B2
Hillborough Cres. PO5 30 D4
Hillbrow Clo. PO9 15 F2
Hillmead Gdns. PO8 20 B3
Hillside Av. PO7 19 E3
Hillside Clo. PO8 8 C4
Hillside Cres. PO6 16 D3
Hillsley Rd. PO6 17 E2
Hilltop Cres. PO6 19 E3
Hilltop Gdns. PO8 8 C4

Hillview. PO8 11 G4
Hilsea Cres. PO2 24 D3
Hiltingbury Rd. PO9 15 E6
Hilton Rd. PO12 28 A5
Hinton Clo. PO9 20 D1
Hinton Daubnay Rd.
PO8 8 A4
Hinton Manor La. PO8 8 C3
Hipley Rd. PO9 21 G2
Hither Grn. PO10 23 H3
Hitherwood Clo. PO7 14 A2
Hobbs Pass. PO12 28 C4
Hobby Clo. PO3 25 E3
Hockham Clo. PO9 14 B4
Hockley Clo. PO6 18 B5
Hodges Clo. PO9 21 G2
Hodsbrook Clo. PO6 18 B4
Holbrook Rd. PO1 26 B5
Holbury Ct. PO9 15 F5
Holcot La. PO3 25 G3
Holdenhurst Clo. PO8 8 C6
Hollam Rd. PO4 31 H1
Holland Rd. PO4 31 E2
Hollow La. PO11 34 B4
Holly Dri. PO7 13 G5
Holly St. PO12 28 A4
Hollybank Clo. PO8 11 G4
Hollybank La. PO10 22 C1
Holman Clo. PO8 13 H1
Holne Ct. PO4 32 B4
Holst Way. PO7 13 F6
Holt Gdns. PO9 9 B5
Holybourne Rd. PO9 21 F2
Holyrood Clo. PO7 13 G4
Holywell Dri. PO6 17 F5
Home Mead. PO7 9 B3
Homefield Path. PO6 19 F6
Homefield Rd,
Cosham. PO6 19 F6
Homefield Rd,
Westbourne. PO10 23 F2
Homefield Way. PO8 8 B1
Homer Clo. PO8 13 F1
Homewell. PO9 21 F4
Honeysuckle Ct. PO7 13 G5
Honeywood Clo. PO3 25 E4
Hooks Farm Way. PO9 20 D2
Hooks La. PO9 20 D2
Hope St. PO1 6 E1
Hopfield Clo. PO7 13 F4
Hopfield Mews. PO7 13 F4
Hopkins Clo. PO6 16 D4
Hordle Rd. PO9 20 C1
Hornbeam Rd. PO9 21 H2
Horndean Rd. PO10 22 B1
Hornet Clo. PO12 28 A5
Horse Sands Clo. PO4 32 C4
Horsea Clo. PO2 24 C3
Horsea Rd. PO2 24 D3
Hospital La. PO16 16 D6
Horsebridge Rd. PO9 21 G1
Houghton Clo. PO9 15 F5
Howard Rd. PO2 24 D3
Hoylake Rd. PO6 19 F4
Hudson Rd. PO5 30 C2
Hulbert Rd,
Bedhampton. PO9 20 B1
Hulbert Rd,
Waterlooville. PO7 13 F3
Huntsman Clo. PO8 10 D4
Hunter Rd,
Cosham. PO6 18 C4
Hunter Rd,
Southsea. PO4 31 G3
Hunters Ride. PO7 13 E4
Huntley Clo. PO6 17 G3
Hurn Ct. PO9 15 F5
Hursley Rd. PO6 14 C6
Hurst Green Clo. PO8 11 F6
Hurstbourne Clo. PO9 14 C5
Hurstville Dri. PO7 13 F5
Hurstwood Rd. PO10 23 H5
Hussar Ct. PO7 12 D2
Hyde Park Rd. PO5 6 F3
Hyde St. PO5 30 B2
Hythe Rd. PO6 18 B5

Ibsley Gro. PO9 20 D2
Icarus Pl. PO7 19 H3
Idsworth Clo. PO8 11 H3
Idsworth Rd,
Portsmouth. PO3 27 F2
Idsworth Rd,
Waterlooville. PO7 14 A1
Ilex Walk. PO11 35 E4
Ilford Ct. PO9 15 F5

James Callaghan Dri.
PO17 17 E1
James Callaghan Way.
PO17 16 D1
James Copse Rd. PO8 10 D4
James Howell Ct. PO7 9 B3
James Rd. PO9 21 E3
Japonica Way. PO9 22 A1
Jaqueline Av. PO7 19 G1
Jarndyce Walk. PO2 26 A3
Jasmine Gro. PO7 13 G5
Jasmine Way. PO8 8 C2
Jasmond Rd. PO6 25 E1
Jason Pl. PO7 19 H3
Jay Clo. PO8 11 E2
Jenkins Gro. PO3 27 G4
Jenner Rd. PO6 18 B4
Jersey Rd. PO2 26 C2
Jervis Rd. PO2 24 B5
Jessica Clo. PO7 13 H2
Jessie Rd,
Bedhampton. PO9 20 C2
Jessie Rd,
Southsea. PO4 31 E2
Jodrell Clo. PO8 11 G2
John King Shipyard.
PO10 22 D6
Joseph St. PO12 28 A4
Jubilee Av. PO6 16 D3
Jubilee Rd,
Portchester. PO16 16 C4
Jubilee Rd,
Southsea. PO4 31 F3
Jubilee Rd,
Waterlooville. PO7 13 E2
Jubilee Ter. PO5 30 B3
Juliet Ct. PO7 13 H3
Juniper Rd. PO8 8 C6
Juniper Sq. PO9 21 F
Jupiter Ct. PO1 6 B4
Jura Clo. PO6 18 C4
Juventu Clo. PO9 21 G2

Karen Av. PO6 25 G1
Kassassin St. PO4 31 H4
Kassel Clo. PO7 14 A3
Katrina Gdns. PO11 34 C2
Kearsney Av. PO2 24 D5
Keats Av. PO6 16 D2
Keats Clo. PO8 10 D5
Keel Clo. PO3 25 G4
Kefford Clo. PO8 11 F3
Kelly Rd. PO7 13 F5
Kelsey Av. PO10 23 H4
Kelsey Head. PO6 17 F4
Kelvin Gro. PO16 16 C3
Kempton Pk. PO7 14 A2
Kemshott Ct. PO9 14 B5
Ken Berry Ct. PO9 15 F5
Kendal Av. PO3 27 E1
Kendal Clo. PO8 11 E5
Kenilworth Rd. PO5 30 D5
Kennedy Clo. PO7 19 G1
Kensington Rd,
Gosport. PO12 28 A5
Kensington Rd,
Portsmouth. PO2 25 E5
Kent Gro. PO16 16 C3
Kent Rd. PO5 30 B3
Kent St. PO1 6 C3
Kentidge Rd. PO7 13 E6
Kenwood Rd. PO16 16 C6
Kenya Rd. PO16 16 A4
Kenyon Rd. PO2 25 E5
Kestrel Clo. PO8 8 C3
Kestrel Pl. PO6 19 H6
Kestrel Pl. PO3 25 F3
Keswick Av. PO3 27 E2
Kettering Ter. PO2 26 A3
Keyhaven Dri. PO9 14 B6
Khandala Gdns. PO7 19 H1
Kidmore La. PO7 9 B1
Kilbride Path. PO2 26 B2
Kilmeston Clo. PO9 14 D5
Kilmiston Clo. PO1 26 C4
Kilmiston Dri. PO16 16 B2
Kiln Rd. PO3 27 F1
Kiln Side. PO7 9 B4
Kilpatrick Clo. PO2 26 B2
Kilwich Way. PO16 16 A6
Kimberley Rd. PO4 31 G4
Kimbolton Rd. PO3 27 E5
Kimbridge Cres. PO9 15 E5
Kimton Ct. PO9 15 F5

41

King Albert St. PO1 26 B5
King Arthurs Ct. PO6 19 G5
King Charles St. PO1 29 F5
*King Edward Ct,
White Hart Rd. PO1 29 E5
King Edwards Cres.
PO2 24 C5
King George Rd. PO16 16 C4
King Henry I St. PO1 6 D3
King John Av. PO16 16 A4
King Richard Clo. PO6 18 A5
King Richard I St. PO1 6 D3
King St,
Emsworth. PO10 22 D6
King St,
Gosport. PO12 28 B3
King St,
Southbourne. PO10 23 E2
King St,
Southsea. PO5 6 E4
King William St. PO1 6 C1
Kingfisher Clo,
Hayling Island. PO11 35 E5
Kingfisher Clo,
Rowlands Castle. PO9 15 F2
Kingfisher Clo,
Wecock. PO8 10 C5
Kingfisher Ct. PO3 25 E3
Kingfisher Dri. PO10 23 F2
Kings Bench Alley. PO1 6 C2
Kings Clo. PO9 15 E1
Kings Mede. PO8 11 E3
Kings Rd,
Cowplain. PO8 10 D6
Kings Rd,
Emsworth. PO10 22 C6
Kings Rd,
Gosport. PO12 28 A3
Kings Rd,
Hayling Island. PO11 34 C1
Kings Rd,
Portsmouth. PO1 6 B1
Kings Rd,
Southsea. PO5 30 B2
Kings Ter,
Emsworth. PO10 22 D5
Kings Ter,
Southsea. PO5 30 B3
Kingsclere Av. PO9 14 C6
Kingscote Rd,
Cowplain. PO8 10 B6
Kingscote Rd,
Paulsgrove. PO6 17 E2
Kingscroft La. PO9 20 D4
Kingsdown Pl. PO1 31 E1
Kingsdown Rd. PO7 12 D1
Kingsland Clo. PO6 17 H3
Kingsley Av. PO10 22 C5
Kingsley Grn. PO9 14 C5
Kingsley Rd. PO4 32 A3
Kingston Cres. PO2 26 B2
Kingston Rd. PO1 26 B1
Kingsway. PO11 36 B2
Kingsworthy Rd. PO9 21 F2
Kinnell Clo. PO12 22 C5
Kinross Cres. PO6 19 E6
Kintyre Rd. PO6 18 C4
Kipling Rd. PO2 24 D4
Kirby Rd. PO2 24 D4
Kirkstall Rd. PO4 30 D6
Kirtley Clo. PO6 25 G1
Kirton Rd. PO6 19 E6
Kite Clo. PO8 10 C5
*Kitwood Grn,
Ropley Rd. PO9 15 F6
Knockin Clo. PO7 13 F4
Knightwood Av. PO9 15 E6
Knowsley Cres. PO6 18 D6
Knowsley Rd. PO6 18 C6
Knox Rd,
Havant. PO9 20 D4
Knox Rd,
Portsmouth. PO2 24 B6

Laburnum Av. PO6 19 F6
Laburnum Gro,
Hayling Island. PO11 34 D3
Laburnum Gro,
Portsmouth. PO2 24 C6
Laburnum Rd. PO7 13 E5
Ladies Mile. PO6 30 C5
Ladybridge Rd. PO7 19 F1
Lake End Dri. PO9 22 C5
Lake Rd. PO1 6 F1
Lakeside Av. PO3 27 F4

Lakeside Gdns. PO9 21 G3
Lakesmere Rd. PO8 11 G3
Lambert Clo. PO7 13 F6
Lampeter Av. PO6 19 E5
Lancaster Clo. PO16 16 A2
Lancaster Way. PO7 13 F5
Landguard Rd. PO4 31 G3
Landport St,
Landport. PO1 26 B5
Landport St,
Southsea. PO5 6 D4
Landport Ter. PO1 6 D4
Landport Vw. PO1 6 F1
Langbrook Clo. PO9 21 F5
Langdale Av. PO6 18 D6
Langford Rd. PO1 26 D3
Langley Rd. PO2 26 C2
Langrish Clo. PO9 15 E5
Langstone Av. PO9 21 F6
Langstone Rd,
Havant. PO9 21 F5
Langstone Rd,
Portsmouth. PO3 27 E5
Lansdowne Av,
Portchester. PO16 16 C6
Lansdowne Av,
Waterlooville. PO7 19 E3
Lansdowne St. PO5 6 D4
Lantana Clo. PO7 13 G5
Lapwing Clo. PO8 11 E2
Lapwing Rd. PO4 27 H6
Larchfield Way. PO8 11 F4
Larchwood Av. PO9 20 B1
Lark Way. PO10 23 F2
Larkhill Rd. PO3 25 E4
*Larkwhistle Walk,
Berrydown Rd. PO9 14 B4
*Lasham Gdns,
Tunworth Ct. PO9 15 F6
*Lasham Grn,
Newnham Ct. PO9 15 F6
Latchmore Forest Gro.
PO8 11 E6
Latchmore Gdns. PO8 10 D6
Latimer Ct. PO3 25 G4
Lauder Clo. PO10 23 H4
Laurel Rd. PO8 11 G4
Laurence Grn. PO10 22 D2
Laurus Clo. PO7 13 G6
Lavant Clo. PO8 13 H2
Lavant Dri. PO9 21 G2
Lavender Rd. PO7 13 G5
Laverock Lea. PO16 16 B3
Lawnswood Clo. PO8 13 G1
Lawrence Av. PO8 10 C6
Lawrence Rd. PO5 31 E4
Lawson Rd. PO5 31 E2
Lazy Acre. PO10 23 G5
Lealand Gro. PO6 19 F5
Lealand Rd. PO6 19 F6
Leckford Clo. PO16 16 B2
Leckford Rd. PO9 15 F5
Ledbury Rd. PO6 17 G3
Legion Rd. PO11 34 C3
Leigh Rd. PO9 21 F3
Leith Av. PO16 16 C3
Lendorber Av. PO6 18 D5
Lennox Lodge. PO11 34 A4
Lennox Rd North. PO5 30 C4
Lennox Rd South. PO5 30 C5
Lennox Row. PO1 6 C1
Lensyd Gdns. PO8 10 D3
Leofric Ct. PO4 32 B4
Leominster Rd. PO6 17 F2
Leonard Rd. PO12 28 A3
Leopold St. PO4 31 E4
Lester Av. PO9 20 D3
Leventhorpe Ct. PO12 28 A4
Lewis Rd. PO10 22 D2
Lexden Gdns. PO11 34 B3
Leyland Clo. PO12 28 A5
Liam Clo. PO9 21 G1
Lichfield Dri. PO9 21 G1
Lichfield Rd. PO3 27 E5
Liddiards Way. PO7 19 H2
Lidiard Gdns. PO4 32 A5
Lightfoot Lawn. PO4 32 B4
Lighthouse Clo. PO11 33 H3
Lilac Clo. PO9 22 A2
Lily Av. PO7 19 E3
Limberline Rd. PO3 25 E3
Limberline Spur. PO3 25 E3
Lime Gro,
Paulsgrove. PO6 17 F2
Lime Gro,
Hayling Island. PO11 33 G3

Lincoln Rise. PO8 11 E5
Lincoln Rd. PO1 26 C6
Lind Clo. PO7 19 H2
Linda Gro. PO8 10 D6
Linden Clo. PO10 22 C3
Linden Gro. PO11 34 C3
Linden Lea. PO16 16 B3
Linden Way,
Havant. PO9 21 F2
Linden Way,
Cowplain. PO8 11 F3
Lindisfarne Clo. PO6 18 D5
Lindley Av. PO4 31 G4
Linford Ct. PO9 14 B4
Link Rd. PO9 20 D1
Linkenholt Way. PO9 20 C1
Linklater Path. PO1 26 B4
Links La. PO9 15 F1
Links Rd. PO11 33 G4
Linnet Clo. PO8 10 C4
Lion St. PO1 6 C2
Lion Ter. PO1 6 D2
Lisle Way. PO10 22 C2
Liss Rd. PO4 31 F2
Lister Rd. PO6 18 B5
Lith Cres. PO8 8 B6
Lith La. PO8 8 B6
Little Arthur St. PO2 26 C3
Little Britain St. PO1 6 C3
Little Coburg St. PO1 26 B5
Little Corner. PO7 9 B4
Little George St. PO1 26 C3
Little Hyden La. PO8 8 B1
Little Mead. PO7 9 C4
Little Southsea St. PO5 30 B3
Littlegreen Av. PO9 21 G2
Littlepark Av. PO9 20 B2
Littleton Gro. PO9 21 F1
Liverpool Rd. PO1 26 C5
Livesay Gdns. PO3 27 E5
Livingstone Rd. PO5 30 D3
Lobelia Ct. PO9 13 G5
Locarno Rd. PO3 25 E5
Lock App. PO6 17 F5
Lock Vw. PO6 17 F4
Lockerley Rd. PO9 21 G2
Locksheath Clo. PO9 14 B5
Locksway Rd. PO4 31 H2
Lodge Av. PO6 18 D5
Lodge Rd. PO9 20 C4
Lodgebury Clo. PO10 23 H5
Lodsworth Clo. PO8 8 C3
Lombard St. PO1 29 F5
Lombardy Rise. PO7 13 G6
Lomond Clo. PO2 26 B2
Londesborough Rd.
PO4 31 E3
London Av. PO2 24 C5
London Rd,
Clanfield. PO8 8 C6
London Rd,
Cowplain. PO8 11 E6
London Rd,
Cosham. PO6 18 C5
London Rd,
Horndean. PO8 11 H2
London Rd,
Portsmouth. PO2 26 B2
London Rd,
Waterlooville. PO7 13 F3
Lone Valley. PO7 19 F2
Long Acre. PO1 26 C4
Long Copse La. PO10 22 C1
Long Curtain Rd. PO1 30 A4
Longdean Clo. PO6 17 E2
Longfield Clo. PO4 27 G6
Longfield Rd. PO10 22 C2
Longlands Rd. PO10 23 G5
Longmead Gdns. PO9 21 F6
Longs Walk. PO1 26 B4
Longshore Way. PO4 32 C3
Longstock Rd. PO9 15 F5
Longwood Av. PO8 10 D5
Lonsdale Av,
Cosham. PO6 18 D6
Lonsdale Av,
Portchester. PO16 16 C6
Lord Montgomery Way.
PO5 6 D3
Lordington Clo. PO6 19 E5
Lords St. PO1 26 B5
Lorne Rd. PO5 31 E2
Lovage Way. PO8 8 C6
Lovedean La. PO8 10 C2
Lovett Rd. PO3 25 E4

Lowcay Rd. PO5 30 D4
Lower Bere Wood. PO7 13 F4
Lower Brookfield Rd.
PO1 26 C5
Lower Church Path. PO1 6 F2
Lower Derby Rd. PO2 24 B6
Lower Drayton La. PO6 19 E6
Lower Farlington Rd.
PO6 19 H5
Lower Forbury Rd.
PO5 30 D1
Lower Grove Rd. PO9 21 G5
Lower Rd. PO9 20 B4
Lower Wingfield St.
PO1 26 A4
Lowestoft Rd. PO6 18 A4
Lowland Rd. PO7 9 A3
Loxwood Rd. PO8 10 D3
Luard Ct. PO9 21 H4
Lucerne Av. PO7 12 D1
Lucknow St. PO1 26 C6
Ludcombe. PO7 9 B2
Ludlow Rd. PO6 18 A4
Lugano Clo. PO7 12 D2
Lulworth Clo. PO11 34 C2
Lumley Gdns. PO10 23 E5
Lumley Rd. PO10 22 D4
Lumsden Rd. PO4 32 C4
Lutman St. PO10 22 C2
Lych Gate Dri. PO6 11 E1
Lydney Clo. PO6 17 H3
Lymbourn Rd. PO9 21 G4
Lyndhurst Clo. PO11 34 C4
Lyndhurst Rd. PO2 24 D5
Lyne Pl. PO8 11 F3
Lynn Rd. PO2 26 D2
Lynton Gro. PO3 27 F2
Lynwood Av. PO8 10 B6
Lysander Ct. PO1 6 B4
Lysander Way. PO7 13 G3

Mablethorpe Rd. PO6 18 A4
Macaulay Av. PO6 17 E2
Madeira Rd. PO2 24 D4
Mafeking Rd. PO4 31 F2
Magdala Rd,
Cosham. PO6 18 C6
Magdala Rd,
Hayling Island. PO11 34 A4
Magdalen Rd. PO2 24 C4
Magnolia Way. PO8 11 F5
Magpie Walk. PO8 10 C5
Maidford Gro. PO3 25 G4
Maidstone Cres. PO6 18 B4
Main Rd,
Portsmouth. PO1 6 A1
Main Rd,
Southbourne. PO10 23 E5
Maismore Gdns. PO10 22 B6
Maitland St. PO1 26 B4
Maldon Rd. PO6 18 A5
Malins Rd. PO2 26 B3
Mallard Rd,
Rowlands Castle. PO9 15 F2
Mallard Rd,
Southsea. PO4 27 F6
Mallard Way. PO10 23 F2
Mallow Clo,
Cosham. PO6 18 C5
Mallow Clo,
Waterlooville. PO7 13 G5
Malta Rd. PO2 26 C3
Malthouse Rd. PO2 26 B2
Malvern Mews. PO4 32 C4
Malvern Rd. PO5 30 D5
Malwood Clo. PO9 15 F5
Manchester Rd. PO1 26 C6
Manners La. PO4 31 E2
Manners Rd. PO4 31 E2
Manor Clo. PO9 21 F4
Manor Cres. PO6 19 E6
Manor Lodge Rd. PO9 15 E1
Manor Mews. PO6 19 E1
Manor Park Av. PO3 27 E2
Manor Rd,
Hayling Island. PO11 34 B3
Manor Rd.,
Portsmouth. PO1 26 C4
Manor Rd,
Southbourne. PO10 23 G5
Manor Way,
Hayling Island. PO11 34 C5
Manor Way,
Southbourne. PO10 23 G5
Mansion Rd. PO4 31 E5

Mansvid Av. PO6 19 E6
Mantle Sq. PO2 24 A6
Maple Clo. PO10 22 D3
Maple Cres. PO8 8 C2
Maple Dri. PO7 9 C3
Maple Rd. PO5 31 E5
Maple Tree Av. PO8 11 F5
Maple Wood. PO9 20 B4
Maralyn Av. PO7 13 F5
Maraxon Rd. PO3 25 F5
Marchwood Rd. PO9 14 C5
Margaret Clo. PO7 13 E2
Margate Rd. PO5 30 C2
Margerys Ct. PO1 6 B3
Marina Clo. PO10 22 D6
Marina Gro,
Portchester. PO16 16 B5
Marina Gro,
Portsmouth. PO3 27 F4
Marina Keep. PO6 24 A1
Marine Ct. PO4 31 H5
Marine Walk. PO11 35 E4
Mariners Walk. PO4 27 G5
Mariners Way. PO12 28 B5
Marion Rd. PO4 31 E5
Marjoram Cres. PO8 11 F5
Mark Anthony Ct.
PO11 34 B4
Mark Clo. PO3 25 E3
Mark Ct. PO7 13 F3
Marker Par. PO9 21 F4
Marketway. PO1 6 E1
Marlands Clo. PO10 22 B5
*Marlands Lawn,
Whaddon Ct. PO9 14 B5
Marlborough Av. PO1 6 B3
Marlborough Clo. PO7 13 E6
Marlborough Gro.
PO16 16 B5
Marlborough Park.
PO9 21 H2
Marlborough Row. PO1 6 B1
Marldell Clo. PO9 15 F5
Marlowe Ct. PO7 13 E2
Marmion Av. PO5 30 D4
Marmion Rd. PO5 30 C4
Marples Way. PO9 20 D4
Marrels Wood. PO7 19 F1
Marsden Rd. PO6 17 G3
Marsh Clo. PO6 25 G1
Marshall Rd. PO11 35 E5
Marshlands Rd. PO6 19 G6
Marshlands Spur. PO6 19 G6
Marshwood Av. PO7 13 H4
Marston La. PO3 25 G4
Martells Ct. PO1 6 C4
Martin Av. PO7 9 C3
Martin Rd,
Havant. PO9 21 G1
Martin Rd,
Portsmouth. PO3 27 E2
Marvic Ct. PO9 14 C5
Masefield Av. PO6 16 D2
Masefield Cres. PO8 10 D5
Matapan Rd. PO2 24 C3
Matthew Clo. PO9 20 C2
Maurepas Way. PO7 13 E4
Maurice Rd. PO4 32 A3
Mavis Cres. PO9 21 F3
Maxstoke Clo. PO5 30 D1
Maxwell Rd. PO4 31 G3
Maughan Sq. PO3 27 E4
Mayfield Av,
Gosport. PO12 28 A5
Mayfield Rd,
Portsmouth. PO2 24 C5
Mayflower Dri. PO4 27 G5
Mayhall Rd. PO3 25 E6
Maylands Av. PO4 31 G1
Maylands Rd. PO9 20 B3
Mayles Rd. PO4 27 G6
Maynard Pl. PO8 11 F2
Mayo Clo. PO1 26 B4
Maytree Gdns. PO6 10 C6
Maytree Rd. PO6 10 C6
Meaden Clo. PO9 15 F6
Meadend Rd. PO7 9 B4
Meadow Clo. PO9 36 A2
Meadow Ct. PO10 22 D5
Meadow Edge. PO7 19 F1
Meadow Rise. PO8 11 F5
Meadow Way,
Havant. PO9 30 B2
Meadowlands,
Havant. PO9 21 G1
Meadowlands,
Rowlands Castle. PO9 9 C5

Meadowsweet. PO7 14 A2
Meadowsweet Way. PO6 18 A4
Meadway. PO7 13 G2
Meath Clo. PO11 35 E6
Medina Rd. PO6 18 A5
Medstead Rd. PO9 21 F2
Melbourne St. PO5 6 E4
Mellor Clo. PO6 18 A5
Melrose Clo. PO4 32 A3
Melville Rd. PO4 32 B4
Mengham Av. PO11 34 C5
Mengham Ct. PO11 34 C4
Mengham La. PO11 34 C4
Mengham Rd. PO11 34 C4
Meon Clo. PO8 8 C3
Meon Rd. PO4 31 H1
Mercator Av. PO1 6 A3
Merchistoun Rd. PO8 11 F2
Mercury Pl. PO7 19 H3
Meredith Rd. PO2 24 D4
Meriden Rd. PO5 6 E4
Merlin Dri. PO3 25 E3
Merlin Gdns. PO16 16 B2
Merrivale Ct. PO10 23 H4
Merrivale Rd. PO2 24 D4
Merrow Clo. PO16 16 A4
Merryfield Av. PO16 14 C6
Merthyr Av. PO6 19 E4
Merton Av. PO16 16 C5
Merton Cres. PO16 16 C5
Merton Rd. PO5 30 C4
Meryl Rd. PO4 32 B3
Methuen Rd. PO4 31 G3
Mewsey Ct. PO9 14 C4
Mey Clo. PO7 13 G4
Meyrick Rd. PO9 20 D4
Meyrick Rd. PO2 24 B6
Michael Crook Clo. PO9 20 C2
Midas Clo. PO7 19 H1
*Middle Ct, George St. PO1 26 C3
Middle Park Way. PO9 14 B6
Middle St. PO5 6 E3
Middlesex Rd. PO4 31 H2
Middleton Rise. PO8 8 C3
Midway Rd. PO2 24 D3
Mika Ct. PO1 6 E3
Milbeck Clo. PO8 11 E6
Mile End Rd. PO2 26 A4
Milebush Rd. PO4 27 G6
Milford Clo. PO9 20 D2
Milford Rd. PO1 26 B6
Military Rd. PO3 24 D2
Military Rd. PO1 29 G1
Milk La F.P. PO7. 12 D5
Mill Clo. PO7 9 C3
Mill End. PO10 23 E5
Mill La, Bedhampton. PO9 20 C4
Mill La, Langstone. PO9 21 F6
Mill La. PO10 23 E4
Mill La. PO7 18 B3
Mill La. PO1 26 A4
Mill Quay. PO10 23 E6
Mill Rd, Denmead. PO7 9 C3
Mill Rd, Waterlooville. PO7 13 E5
Mill Rd, Westbourne'. PO10 23 F1
Millbrook Dri. PO9 15 E5
Mills Rd. PO2 26 B2
Milton La. PO3 26 D6
Milton Parade. PO7 13 E1
Milton Park Av. PO4 31 H2
Milton Rd, Cowplain. PO8 10 D5
Milton Rd, Portsmouth. PO3 27 E4
Milton Rd, Waterlooville. PO7 13 E2
Minerva Clo. PO7 19 H3
Minerva Cres. PO1 6 B4
Minley Ct. PO9 15 F6
Minnitt Rd. PO12 28 C4
Minstead Rd. PO4 32 A4
Minters Lepe. PO7 19 G2
Mission La. PO8 10 D6
Mitchell Rd. PO9 20 C2
Mitchell Way. PO3 25 G4
Mole Hill. PO7 13 G6
Molesworth Rd. PO12 28 A5
Monarch Clo. PO7 13 G4

Monckton Rd. PO3 25 E5
Moneyfields Av. PO3 27 E2
Moneyfields La. PO3 27 E2
Monks Hill. PO10 23 E1
Monkwood Clo. PO9 14 B6
Monmouth Clo. PO7 13 G4
Monmouth Rd. PO2 24 C6
Montague Rd. PO2 24 C6
Montana Ct. PO7 13 G5
Monteray Dri. PO9 21 G1
Montgomerie Rd. PO5 30 D2
Montgomery Rd. PO9 21 G4
Montgomery Wk. PO7 12 D6
Monton Ct. PO9 15 F5
Montrose Av. PO16 16 D2
Monument La. PO17 16 B1
*Monxton Grn, Burghclere Rd. PO9 15 F5
Moor Park. PO7 14 A2
Moorgreen Rd. PO9 15 E6
Moorings Way. PO4 27 G5
Moorland Rd. PO1 26 C5
Moortown Av. PO6 19 F4
Moraunt Dri. PO16 16 A5
Morelands Ct. PO7 19 H1
Morelands Rd. PO7 19 G1
Morgan Rd. PO4 32 A3
Morley Cres. PO8 11 E5
Morley Rd. PO4 31 G4
Morningside Av. PO16 16 D3
Mortimer Rd. PO6 17 G3
Mortimers Lawn. PO9 14 C4
Mosdell Rd. PO10 23 H6
Moulin Av. PO5 31 E4
Mount View Av. PO16 16 D3
*Mountbatten Sq, Gunners Row. PO4 32 A5
Mountwood Rd. PO16 23 H4
Mousehole Rd. PO6 17 E3
Muccleshell Clo. PO9 21 G1
Mulberry Av. PO6 18 D6
Mulberry La. PO6 18 D6
Mulberry Path. PO6 18 D6
Mullion Clo. PO6 17 G5
Mumby Rd. PO12 28 B3
Mundays Row. PO8 8 C6
Munster Rd. PO2 24 C5
Murefield St. PO1 26 B6
Muriel Rd. PO7 13 F3
Murray Rd. PO8 11 F3
Murrays La. PO1 6 A1
*Murrel Gdns, Tunworth Ct. PO9 15 F6
*Murrell Grn, Meaden Clo. PO9 15 F6
Muscliffe Ct. PO9 15 F5
Museum Rd. PO1 30 A2
My Lords La. PO9 34 D4
Myrtle Av. PO16 16 C4
Myrtle Gro. PO3 27 F4
Nailsworth Rd. PO6 17 G3
Naish Ct. PO9 14 B4
Nancy Rd. PO1 26 C6
Napier Rd, Horndean. PO8 11 G2
Napier Rd, Southsea. PO5 30 D4
Narvik Rd. PO2 24 C3
Naseby Clo. PO6 17 F3
Navy Rd. PO1 29 F1
Neelands Gro. PO6 16 D4
Nelson Av, Portchester. PO16 16 A4
Nelson Av, Portsmouth. PO2 24 C5
Nelson Cres. PO8 11 F2
Nelson La. PO17 16 B1
Nelson Rd, Portsmouth. PO1 26 A4
Nelson Rd, Southsea. PO5 30 C3
Neptune Ct. PO1 6 B4
Nerissa Clo. PO7 13 H2
Nessus St. PO2 26 B2
Netherfield Clo. PO9 21 G4
Netley Rd. PO5 30 C4
Netley Ter. PO5 30 C4
Nettlecombe Av. PO4 31 E5
Nettlestone Rd. PO4 31 G4
Neville Av. PO16 16 C5
Neville Gdns. PO10 22 C2
Neville Rd. PO3 27 F4
Neville Shute Rd. PO3 25 F4
New Brighton Rd. PO10 22 D4

New Cut. PO11 36 A2
New Down La. PO7 18 D3
New La. PO9 21 G3
New Rd, Clanfield. PO8 8 C3
New Rd, Havant. PO9 20 D3
New Rd, Lovedean. PO8 10 C2
New Rd, Portsmouth. PO2 26 C3
New Rd, Southbourne. PO10 23 H5
New Rd, Westbourne. PO10 23 E2
New Rd East. PO2 26 D3
Newbarn Rd. PO9 20 C2
Newbolt Gdns. PO8 10 C5
Newbolt Rd. PO6 16 D3
Newcome Rd. PO1 26 C5
Newcomen Rd. PO2 24 B6
Newlands La. PO7 12 B3
Newlands Rd. PO7 13 E6
Newlease Rd. PO7 13 F6
Newlyn Way. PO6 17 F4
Newmer Ct. PO9 14 B5
Newney Clo. PO9 25 E4
Newnham Ct. PO9 15 F6
Newtown. PO16 16 C4
Newtown La. PO11 34 A3
Nicholas Ct. PO11 34 A4
Nicholson Way. PO9 21 E2
Nickel St. PO5 30 B3
Nickleby Rd. PO8 8 B1
Nightjar Clo. PO8 11 F2
Nightingale Clo. PO9 15 F2
Nightingale Pk. PO10 13 F2
Nightingale Pk. PO9 21 H4
Nightingale Rd. PO5 30 B4
Nile St. PO10 22 D6
Ninian Park Rd. PO3 25 E5
Ninian Path. PO3 25 E5
Nobbs La. PO1 6 C4
Nore Cres. PO10 22 B5
Nore Farm Av. PO10 22 B4
Norfolk Cres. PO11 34 A5
Norfolk Rd. PO5 30 B2
Norgett Way. PO16 16 B5
Norland Rd. PO4 31 E2
Norley Clo. PO9 14 C6
Norman Clo. PO16 16 C5
Norman Rd, Hayling Island. PO11 34 D5
Norman Rd, Southsea. PO4 31 E3
Norman Way. PO9 20 C3
Normandy Rd. PO7 24 C3
Norris Gdns. PO9 21 G5
North Av. PO2 24 D4
North Battery Rd. PO2 24 A5
North Clo. PO9 21 G5
*North Ct, George St. PO2 26 C3
North Cres. PO11 34 D4
North Cross St. PO12 28 C4
North End Av. PO2 24 C6
North End Gro. PO2 24 C5
North La. PO8 8 B1
North Rd. PO8 8 C5
North Shore Rd. PO11 33 H3
North St, Bedhampton. PO9 20 D3
North St, Emsworth. PO10 22 D4
North St, Gosport. PO12 28 B3
North St, Havant. PO9 21 F4
North St, Portsea. PO1 6 C2
North St, Portsmouth. PO1 26 B4
North St, Westbourne. PO10 23 E2
North Way. PO9 21 E4
Northam Mews. PO1 26 B5
Northam St. PO1 26 B5
Northarbour Path. PO6 18 A6
Northarbour Rd. PO6 18 A6
Northarbour Spur. PO6 18 A6
Northbrook Clo. PO6 26 B4
Northcote Rd. PO4 31 E3
Northern Par. PO2 24 C4
Northern Rd. PO6 18 C6
Northfield Pk. PO16 16 A3
Northgate Av. PO2 26 B4
Northney La. PO11 36 C1
Northney Rd. PO11 36 B1

Northover Rd. PO3 27 F2
Northumberland Rd. PO1 31 E1
Northwood La. PO11 34 B4
Northwood Rd. PO2 24 D3
Norton Clo. PO7 13 E4
Norway Rd. PO3 25 E3
Norwich Rd. PO6 18 A4
Novello Gdns. PO7 13 F5
Nursery Clo. PO10 22 D2
Nursery Gdns. PO8 11 E4
Nursery Rd. PO9 20 C3
Nursing Cres. PO9 15 F6
Nutbourne Rd, Farlington. PO6 19 G6
Nutbourne Rd, Hayling Island. PO11 35 G5
Nutfield Pl. PO1 26 B4
Nuthatch Clo. PO9 15 F2
Nutley Rd. PO9 14 C6
Nutwick Rd. PO9 21 H2
Nyewood Av. PO16 16 C2
Nyria Wk. PO12 28 B4

Oak Clo. PO8 13 F1
Oak Park Dri. PO9 21 G2
Oak Rd. PO9 20 C3
Oak Rd. PO8 8 C2
Oak St. PO12 28 A4
Oak Tree Dri. PO9 22 C1
Oakapple Gdns. PO6 19 H5
Oakcroft La. PO9 15 F6
Oakhurst Dri. PO7 13 G3
Oakhurst Gdns. PO7 19 E3
Oaklands Gro. PO9 10 C5
Oaklands Rd. PO9 21 G4
Oaklea Clo. PO7 19 E3
Oakmeadow Clo. PO10 22 D2
Oakmont Dri. PO8 13 G1
Oakshott Dri. PO9 15 E5
Oakwood Av. PO9 20 B2
Oakwood Rd,, Hayling Island. PO11 34 B4
Oakwood Rd, Portsmouth. PO2 24 D3
Oberon Clo. PO7 13 G3
Ockenden Clo. PO5 6 E4
Octavius Ct. PO7 13 H2
Old Barn Gdns. PO8 10 D3
Old Bridge Rd. PO4 31 E4
Old Commercial Rd. PO1 26 A4
Old Copse Rd. PO9 21 G2
Old Farm La. PO10 23 F3
Old Farm Way. PO6 19 H6
Old Gate Gdns. PO2 24 D4
Old Lane. PO8 8 B5
Old London Rd. PO2 25 E3
Old Manor Way. PO6 18 D6
Old Rectory Clo. PO10 23 E2
Old Rectory Rd. PO9 19 H5
Old Reservoir Rd. PO6 19 G6
Old River. PO7 9 B3
Old Road. PO12 28 A5
Old School Dri. PO11 34 D5
Old Star Pl. PO1 6 B2
Old Timbers. PO11 34 B4
Old Van Diemans Rd. PO7 12 D6
Old Wymering La. PO6 18 B5
Olinda St. PO1 26 C5
Olive Cres. PO16 16 C5
Oliver Rd. PO4 31 G3
Olivia Clo. PO7 13 H2
Omega St. PO5 30 D1
Onslow Rd. PO5 30 D1
Opal Ct. PO4 31 G2
Ophir Rd. PO2 24 C5
Oracle Dri. PO7 19 H2
Orange Row. PO10 22 D6
Orchard Clo. PO8 11 G3
Orchard Gro, Cowplain. PO8 10 D6
Orchard Gro, Portchester. PO16 16 A5
Orchard La. PO10 23 E5
Orchard Rd, Havant. PO9 21 F5
Orchard Rd, Hayling Island. PO11 34 C5
Orchard Rd, Southsea. PO4 31 E1
Ordnance Ct. PO3 25 F4
Ordnance Ct. PO12 28 B4
Ordnance Row. PO1 6 B3

Oriel Rd. PO2 24 C5
Orkney Rd. PO6 18 C4
Ormsby Rd. PO5 30 C4
Orsmond Clo. PO7 13 F5
Osborne Clo. PO7 13 G4
Osborne Rd. PO5 30 B4
Osprey Clo. PO6 19 H6
Osprey Dri. PO11 34 D4
Osprey Quay. PO10 23 E6
Othello Dri. PO7 13 G3
Otterbourne Cres. PO9 14 C6
Outram Rd. PO3 30 D3
Overton Cres. PO9 14 B6
Overton Rd. PO10 23 H4
Owen St. PO4 31 G4
Owslebury Gro. PO9 14 D6
Oxenwood Grn. PO9 14 B5
Oxford Rd. PO5 31 E4
Oxted Ct. PO4 27 G4
Oyster Mews. PO1 29 F5
Oyster Quay. PO6 17 G5
Oyster St. PO1 29 F5

Padbury Clo. PO2 25 E4
Paddington Rd. PO2 26 D1
Paddock End. PO7 9 B4
Paddock Walk. PO6 17 E4
Padnell Av. PO8 11 F6
Padnell Pl. PO8 11 F6
Padnell Rd. PO8 11 E6
Padwick Av. PO6 18 D5
Pagham Clo. PO10 23 E5
Pagham Gdns. PO11 35 G5
Paignton Av. PO3 27 E2
Pains Rd. PO5 30 C2
Painswick Clo. PO6 17 G3
Painter Clo. PO3 25 G4
Palk Rd. PO9 20 D4
Palmers Rd. PO10 22 D5
Palmerston Rd, Hayling Island. PO11 34 C3
Palmerston Rd, Southsea. PO5 30 C5
Pamela Av. PO6 17 E3
Pan St. PO1 6 F1
Pangbourne Av. PO6 18 D6
Panton Clo. PO10 22 C2
*Parade Vw Mansions, Royal Gate. PO4 31 H4
Paradise La. PO10 23 E1
Paradise St. PO1 6 F2
Parham Rd. PO2 28 A2
Park Av. PO7 19 E3
Park Cres. PO10 22 B5
Park Farm Rd. PO7 19 F1
Park Gro. PO6 18 C6
Park House Farm Way. PO9 14 A6
Park La, Cosham. PO6 18 D5
Park La, Cowplain. PO8 14 A1
Park La, Havant. PO9 20 C3
Park La, Leigh Park. PO9 14 A3
Park Par. PO9 21 F1
Park Rd, Denmead. PO7 9 B2
Park Rd, Hayling Island. PO11 33 G3
Park Rd, Portsmouth. PO1 6 C3
Park Rd, Purbrook. PO7 19 F1
Park Rd, Southbourne. PO10 23 G4
Park Rd North. PO9 21 F3
Park Rd South. PO9 21 F4
Park Side. PO9 20 C3
Park St. PO5 6 D4
Park Way. PO9 21 E4
Parker Gdns. PO7 19 F3
Parklands Av. PO8 11 E4
Parkstone Av. PO4 31 E5
Parkstone La. PO4 31 E5
Parr Rd. PO6 18 A5
Parry Clo. PO6 18 A5
Parsons Clo. PO3 25 E3
*Passfield Walk, Exton Rd. PO9 15 F6
Partridge Gdns. PO8 10 C5
Passingham Walk. PO9 11 E5
Pasteur Rd. PO6 18 B5
Paulsgrove Rd. PO2 26 D2
Peacock La. PO1 30 A3
Peak Rd. PO8 8 A2
Peakfield. PO7 9 A3
Pearce Ct. PO12 28 B4
Pebble Clo. PO11 34 D5
Pebmarsh Rd. PO6 18 B5

Pedam Clo. PO4 31 G3
Peel Rd. PO12 28 A3
Pelham Rd. PO5 30 C3
Pelham Ter. PO10 22 D5
Pembroke Clo. PO1 30 A3
Pembroke Rd. PO1 30 A3
Pembury Rd. PO9 21 G5
Penarth Av. PO6 19 E5
Pendenis Rd. PO6 17 E3
Penhale Rd. PO1 26 C6
Penhurst Rd. PO9 20 B3
Penjar Av. PO7 19 F1
Penk Ridge. PO9 20 A4
Pennant Hills. PO9 20 B3
Penner Rd. PO9 21 E6
Pennerley Ct. PO9 14 B4
Penny La. PO10 23 F5
Penny Pl. PO7 19 H2
Penny St. PO1 29 F5
Penrhyn Av. PO6 19 E5
Penrose Clo. PO2 24 C6
Pentere Rd. PO8 11 E2
Pentland Rise. PO16 16 C2
Penton Ct. PO9 15 G5
*Penwood Gdns,
Stockbridge Clo.
PO9 15 F6
*Penwood Grn,
Minley Ct. PO9 15 F6
Peper Harow. PO8 11 F3
Pepys Clo. PO4 31 F3
Percival Rd. PO2 26 D2
Percy Chandler St.
PO1 26 A5
Percy Rd,
Gosport. PO12 28 A4
Percy Rd,
Southsea. PO4 31 E2
Perrone Clo. PO3 25 E3
Perrone Rd. PO3 25 E3
Perseus Pl. PO7 19 H2
Perseus Ter. PO1 6 B4
Perth Clo. PO12 28 A4
Perth Rd. PO4 32 A3
Pervin Rd. PO6 18 C6
Peter Ashley La. PO6 19 G4
Peterborough Rd. PO6 18 B4
Petersfield Rd,
Clanfield. PO8 8 B1
Petersfield Rd,
Havant. PO9 21 F3
Petersham Clo. PO7 12 D2
Petworth Rd. PO3 27 F5
Philip Av. PO1 6 B3
Philip Rd. PO7 13 F6
Phoenix Sq. PO2 24 D3
Pier Rd. PO1 30 A4
Pigeon House La. PO6 18 A2
Pine Ct. PO10 22 D1
Pine Dri. PO8 8 C3
Pine Gro. PO9 21 G4
Pine Tree Gdns. PO8 13 H1
Pinehurst Clo. PO7 14 A1
Pinewood Av. PO9 20 B2
Pink Rd. PO2 26 C2
Pipers Mead. PO8 11 E2
Pipit Clo. PO8 11 E2
Pitcairn Mews. PO4 32 A5
Pitcroft La. PO2 26 B2
Pitcroft Rd. PO2 26 B2
Pitreavie Rd. PO6 25 E1
Place Cres. PO7 13 F6
Plaitford Gro. PO9 20 C1
Playfair Rd. PO5 30 D2
Pleasant Rd. PO2 32 A3
Plover Reach. PO4 27 F6
Plover Rd. PO8 11 E2
Plumley Walk. PO9 14 B4
Plumpton Gdns. PO3 25 G4
Plumpton Gro. PO7 14 A2
Plymouth St. PO5 6 F3
Pond La. PO8 8 B1
Pond Piece. PO7 9 B3
Pook La. PO9 21 G6
Popham Ct. PO9 15 F6
Poplar Gro. PO11 34 D3
Port Royal St. PO5 30 D1
Port Way. PO6 24 A1
Portchester Heights.
PO16 16 C2
Portchester La. PO17 16 C1
Portchester Rd,
Portchester. PO16 16 A3
Portchester Rd,
Portsmouth. PO2 26 C2
Portfield Rd. PO3 25 F5

Portland Rd,
Southsea. PO5 30 C4
Portland Rd,
Waterlooville. PO7 13 E4
Portland St. PO1 6 C2
Portobello Gro. PO16 16 C3
Portsdown Av. PO6 19 F5
Portsdown Hill Rd,
Cosham. PO6 18 B3
Portsdown Hill Rd,
Fareham. PO17 16 A1
Portsdown Hill Rd,
Havant. PO9 20 A4
Portsdown Rd.,
Portchester PO16 16 D4
Portsdown Rd,
Portsmouth. PO6 16 D4
Portsmouth Rd,
Cosham. PO6 25 E1
Portsmouth Rd,
Horndean. PO8 11 F4
Portsview Av. PO16 16 C3
Portsview Gdns. PO16 16 C3
Portswood Rd,
Leigh Park. PO9 14 B5
Portswood Rd,
Portsmouth. PO2 24 D3
Posbrooke Rd. PO4 31 H1
Post Office Rd. PO7 12 D6
Postern Clo. PO16 16 C4
Poulner Ct. PO9 14 B5
Pound Lea. PO11 34 C2
Power Rd. PO1 26 C4
Powerscourt Rd. PO2 26 B2
Poynings Pl. PO4 29 F5
Preston Rd. PO2 26 D2
Pretoria Rd. PO4 31 F3
*Prettyjohn House,
Gunners Row. PO4 32 A5
Primrose Ct. PO7 13 G5
Prince Albert Rd. PO4 31 G4
Prince George St. PO1 6 C2
Prince Georges St. PO9 21 F4
Prince of Wales Clo.
PO7 13 G4
Prince of Wales Rd.
PO12 28 B4
Princes Dri. PO7 13 G2
Princes Pl. PO1 26 A3
Princes St. PO1 26 A3
Princess Gdns. PO6 11 F2
Prinsted Cres. PO6 19 G6
Prinsted La. PO10 23 G6
Priors Clo. PO10 23 H5
Priorsdean Av. PO3 27 E5
Priorsdean Cres. PO9 20 D1
Priory Cres. PO4 31 G2
Priory Gdns. PO7 13 F2
Priory Rd. PO4 31 G4
Privett Rd. PO7 19 F2
Prochurch Rd. PO8 11 E4
Proctor La. PO1 26 D6
Prospect La. PO9 15 F6
Prospect Rd. PO1 26 A3
Puffin Walk. PO8 10 B5
Pump La. PO8 11 E4
Purbeck St. PO1 6 C3
Purbrook Chase Precinct.
PO7 19 H2
Purbrook Gdns. PO7 12 D6
Purbrook Heath Rd.
PO7 12 A6
Purbrook Rd. PO6 26 C6
Purbrook Way. PO9 20 A1
Purcell Clo. PO7 13 F6
Pycroft Clo. PO11 36 C2
Pye St. PO1 6 F1
Pyle Clo. PO8 11 E5
Pyrford Clo. PO7 13 E1

Quail Way. PO8 11 E2
Quarely Rd. PO9 14 B5
Quartremaine Rd. PO3 25 F4
Queen Annes Dri. PO9 20 C3
Queen Mary Rd. PO16 16 C4
Queen St,
Emsworth. PO10 22 D6
Queen St,
Portsea. PO1 6 B2
Queens Cres,
Horndean. PO8 11 F2
Queens Cres,
Southsea. PO5 30 C4
Queens Gro,
Southsea. PO5 30 C4

Queens Gro,
Waterlooville. PO7 13 E6
Queens Pl. PO5 30 C3
Queens Rd,
Gosport. PO12 28 A3
Queens Rd,
Portsea. PO1 6 A1
Queens Rd,
Portsmouth. PO2 26 B2
Queens Rd,
Waterlooville. PO7 13 F2
Queens Way,
Southsea. PO5 30 C4
Queensway,
Hayling Island. PO11 36 B2
Quinton Clo. PO5 30 D1
Quintrell Av. PO16 16 A4
Race Course La. PO6 17 G4
Racton Av. PO6 19 E6
Racton Rd. PO10 22 D2
Radnor St. PO5 6 F4
Raglan St. PO5 30 D1
Rails La. PO11 34 D4
Railway Vw. PO1 6 F2
Ramblers Way. PO7 14 A2
Rampart Gdns. PO3 24 D2
Rampart Row. PO12 28 C5
Ramsdale Av. PO9 14 A5
Ramsey Rd. PO11 34 C4
Randolph Rd. PO2 24 D4
Ranelagh Rd,
Havant. PO9 20 D4
Ranelagh Rd,
Portsmouth. PO2 24 B6
Range Grn. PO2 24 B4
Rapson Clo. PO6 18 A4
Ravenswood Gdns.
PO5 30 D5
Raymond Rd. PO6 16 D3
Record Rd. PO10 22 C5
Rectory Av. PO6 19 H4
Rectory Rd. PO9 21 F5
Red Lynch Clo. PO9 21 H1
Redbarn Av. PO16 16 B3
Redbridge Gro. PO9 20 D2
Redcar Av. PO3 27 F1
Redcliff Gdns. PO4 31 E6
Redhill Rd. PO9 15 F2
Redlands Gro. PO4 32 B3
Redlands La. PO10 22 D2
Redshank Rd. PO8 11 E2
Redwing Ct. PO4 27 G6
Redwing Rd. PO8 8 C3
Redwood Dri. PO16 16 A3
Redwood Gro. PO9 21 G1
Reedling Dri. PO4 27 H6
Reedmace Clo. PO7 13 G4
Regal Clo. PO6 18 C5
Regency Gdns. PO7 13 E5
Regent Pl. PO5 30 B3
Regent St. PO1 26 A3
Regents Ct. PO9 21 F5
Reginald Rd. PO4 31 G3
Relay Rd. PO7 13 E3
Renny Rd. PO1 26 C6
Renown Gdns. PO8 10 D4
Rest a Wyle Av. PO11 34 C2
Revenge Clo. PO4 27 H5
Rhinefield Clo. PO9 20 C1
Richmond Clo. PO11 34 A3
Richmond Dri. PO11 34 A3
Richmond Pl,
Portsmouth. PO1 6 C3
Richmond Pl,
Southsea. PO5 30 C4
Richmond Rise. PO16 16 B3
Richmond Rd. PO5 30 D4
Riders Grn. PO9 21 E1
Riders La. PO9 14 C6
Ridge Clo. PO8 8 C3
Ridgeway. PO6 17 E2
Rimington Rd. PO8 10 C6
Ringwood Rd. PO4 32 A4
Ripley Gro. PO3 27 F2
Ripon Gdns. PO7 14 A2
Ritchie Clo. PO11 34 C4
Ritson Way. PO9 21 F3
River St. PO10 23 E1
River Way. PO9 21 G2
Riverdale Av. PO7 13 G4
Riverhead Clo. PO9 27 G6
Rivers Rd. PO5 30 C1
Riversdale Gdns. PO9 21 F3

*Riverside Ter,
Spring Gdns. PO10 22 D5
Road Vw. PO1 26 A2
Roads Hill. PO8 8 A6
Robin Gdns. PO8 10 B5
Robinia Clo. PO7 13 G4
Robinson Ct. PO16 16 B3
Robinson Way. PO3 25 G5
Rochester Rd. PO4 31 F3
Rochford Rd. PO6 18 A5
Rockes Clo. PO8 11 F3
Rockingham Way.
PO16 19 G5
Rocksbourne Clo. PO9 20 C1
Rockville Dri. PO7 13 E4
Rodney Rd. PO3 27 E6
Rodney Way. PO8 11 F2
Roebuck Clo. PO6 18 C6
Rogate Gdns. PO16 16 B2
Rogers Mead. PO11 36 A3
Roland Clo. PO8 11 F3
Roman Grn. PO7 9 A3
Roman Gro. PO16 16 C5
Roman Way. PO9 20 C3
Romsey Av. PO3 27 F5
Romsey Rd. PO8 8 C4
Rooksbury Croft. PO9 15 E6
Rookwood View. PO7 9 B2
Ropley Rd. PO9 15 F6
Rose Hill. PO8 11 E3
Rosebay Ct. PO7 13 G6
Rosebery Av. PO6 18 D6
Roselands. PO8 11 E4
Rosemary La. PO1 6 B3
Rosemary Way. PO8 11 F4
Rosetta Rd. PO4 32 A3
Rosewood Gdns. PO8 8 C2
Rosina Clo. PO7 14 A3
Rostrevor La. PO4 31 E5
Rotherwick Clo. PO9 15 F5
Rothwell Clo. PO6 17 F3
Round Way. PO7 13 G3
Roundhouse Mdw.
PO10 23 E6
Rowan Av. PO8 13 H1
Rowan Ct. PO4 31 F2
Rowan Rd. PO9 21 H2
Rowbury Rd. PO9 14 C5
Rowin Clo. PO11 35 F5
Rowland Rd. PO6 16 D3
Rowlands Av. PO7 13 F2
Rowlands Castle Rd.
PO8 11 H3
Rownhams Rd. PO9 14 B6
Royal Gdns. PO9 15 F2
Royal Gate. PO4 31 H4
Royal Way. PO7 13 G4
Rudgwick Clo. PO6 16 A4
Rudmore Pass. PO1 26 A2
Rudmore Rd. PO1 26 A2
Rudmore Sq. PO1 26 A2
Rugby Rd. PO5 31 E2
*Rushmere Walk,
Portswood Rd. PO9 14 B5
Ruskin Rd. PO4 31 G1
Ruskin Way. PO8 10 D5
Russell Rd. PO9 21 F2
Russett Gdns. PO10 23 E5
Rycroft. PO9 21 H4
Rydal Clo. PO7 17 G3

Sackville St. PO5 6 E4
Sadlers Walk. PO10 23 E5
Sage Clo. PO7 13 G5
St Albans Rd. PO9 21 G1
St Albans Rd. PO4 31 G3
St Andrew Clo. PO8 8 C5
St Andrews Rd,
Farlington. PO6 19 H5
St Andrews Rd,
Hayling Island. PO11 34 D5
St Andrews Rd,
Southsea. PO5 30 D3
St Anns Rd,
Horndean. PO8 11 G2
St Anns Rd,
Southsea. PO4 31 F3
St Aubins Pk. PO11 34 H3
St Augustines Rd. PO4 31 F4
St Barbara Way. PO2 25 E3
St Bartholomews Gdns.
PO5 30 D3
St Catherine St. PO5 30 D5
St Catherines Rd.
PO11 33 G4
St Chads Av. PO2 24 D5

St Christophers Rd.
PO9 20 C2
St Clares Av. PO9 14 B4
St Colmans Av. PO6 18 D5
St Davids Rd,
Clanfield. PO8 8 C3
St Davids Rd,
Southsea. PO5 30 D2
*St Denys Walk,
Stanswood Rd. PO9 14 C5
St Edwards Rd. PO5 30 D3
St Faiths Rd. PO1 6 F1
St Francis Pl. PO9 21 E2
St Georges Av. PO9 21 H4
St Georges Rd,
Cosham. PO6 18 C5
St Georges Rd,
Southsea. PO4 31 G5
St Georges Rd,
Hayling Island. PO11 33 H4
St Georges Rd,
Portsmouth. PO1 6 C3
St Georges Sq. PO1 6 C3
St Georges Walk. PO7 13 E4
St Georges Way. PO1 6 C3
St Giles Way. PO8 8 C5
St Helena Way. PO16 16 B4
St Helens Clo. PO4 31 F5
St Helens Par. PO4 31 E5
St Helens Park Cres.
PO4 31 E5
St Helens Rd,. PO11 33 H4
St Hellens Rd. PO6 19 F5
St Hermans Rd. PO11 35 E5
St Hilda Av. PO9 8 C5
St Hubert Rd. PO8 8 C5
St James Clo. PO8 8 C5
St James Rd. PO10 22 D5
St James's Rd. PO5 6 E4
St James's St. PO1 6 C2
St James Way. PO16 16 B4
St Johns Av. PO7 19 G1
St Johns Clo. PO11 34 B4
St Johns Rd,
Cosham. PO6 18 C5
St Johns Rd,
Havant. PO9 20 C1
St Johns Rd,
Southbourne. PO10 23 G5
St Judes Clo. PO5 30 C4
St Leonards Av. PO11 34 C3
St Margarets Rd. PO11 34 C4
St Marks Rd. PO2 24 C6
St Marys Rd,
Hayling Island. PO11 34 C3
St Marys Rd,
Portsmouth. PO1 26 C4
St Matthews Rd. PO6 18 C5
St Michaels Rd,
Bedhampton. PO9 20 C1
St Michaels Rd,
Portsmouth. PO1 6 D3
St Michaels Way. PO8 8 C5
St Nicholas Rd. PO9 20 C2
St Nicholas St. PO1 30 A3
St Pauls Rd. PO5 6 D4
St Pauls Sq. PO5 6 D4
St Peters Av. PO11 36 C3
St Peters Gro. PO5 36 C3
St Peters Rd. PO11 36 C2
St Peters Sq. PO10 22 D5
St Pirans Av. PO3 27 E3
St Ronans Av. PO4 31 E4
St Ronans Rd. PO4 31 E5
St Simons Rd. PO5 30 D5
St Stephens Rd. PO2 26 C2
St Swithuns Rd. PO2 25 E5
St Theresas Clo. PO9 20 D2
St Thomas Av. PO11 33 H4
St Thomas's Ct. PO1 30 A3
St Thomas's St. PO1 6 C4
St Ursula Gro. PO5 30 D3
St Vincent Cres. PO8 11 F2
St Vincent Rd. PO5 30 D4
St Vincent St. PO5 6 E3
Salcombe Av. PO3 27 F2
Salerno Rd. PO2 24 C3
Salisbury Rd,
Cosham. PO6 18 D6
Salisbury Rd,
Southsea. PO4 31 F4
Salterns Av. PO4 27 F5
Salterns Clo. PO11 35 E4
Salterns Clo. PO11 35 E4
Salterns La. PO11 34 A2

Whitworth Rd. PO2	27 E2	Wilson Rd. PO2	24 B5	Winston Churchill Av.		Woodlands Av. PO10	22 C3	Wrexham Gro. PO8	8 B4
Wickham St. PO1	6 B2	Wilton Dri. PO8	11 E3	PO1	6 E3	Woodlands Gro. PO7	13 E6	Wyborn Clo. PO11	34 C5
Wickor Way. PO10	22 D3	Wilton Pl. PO5	30 C4	Winston Clo. PO11	34 A4	Woodlands La. PO11	34 B2	Wyeford Clo. PO9	15 G5
Wicor Mill La. PO16	16 A5	Wilton Ter. PO5	30 C4	Winter Rd. PO4	31 G3	Woodlands Way. PO9	21 F1	Wykeham Av. PO2	24 D6
Wicor Path. PO16	16 A6	Winchcombe Rd. PO6	17 G2	Winterbourne Rd. PO6	17 E2	Woodley Rd. PO12	28 A5	Wykeham Rd. PO2	24 D6
Wicor Path. PO16	16 C6	Wiltshire St. PO5	6 D4	Winterhill Rd. PO6	18 A5	Woodmancote Rd.		Wyllie Rd. PO2	24 D3
Widley Court Dri. PO6	18 D6	Wilverley Av. PO9	21 G1	Winterslow Dri. PO9	14 C5	PO4	31 G2	Wymering La. PO6	18 B5
Widley Gdns. PO7	19 G2	Wimbledon Park Rd.		Winton Rd. PO2	25 E6	Woodpath. PO5	30 C3	Wymering Manor Clo.	
Widley Rd,		PO5	30 D4	Wisborough Rd. PO5	30 D4	Woodpecker Clo. PO9	21 H4	PO6	18 A5
Cosham. PO6	18 D5	Wimborne Rd. PO4	31 G2	Wises Alley. PO12	28 C4	Woodpecker Way. PO3	25 E4	Wymering Rd. PO2	26 C2
Widley Rd,		Wimpole St. PO1	26 B5	Wish Pl. PO5	31 E4	Woodrow. PO7	9 A2	Wyndcliffe Rd. PO4	31 E3
Portsmouth. PO2	24 B5	Wincanton Way. PO7	14 A2	Wisteria Gdns. PO9	21 H1	Woodruffe Walk. PO10	22 D2	Wyndham Clo. PO8	11 F4
Widley Walk. PO7	18 C3	Winchester Rd. PO2	26 C2	Withampton Clo. PO9	15 E6	Woodsedge. PO7	13 G5	Wyndham Mws. PO1	29 F5
Wield Clo. PO9	20 C1	Winchfield Cres. PO9	20 C1	Withington Clo. PO6	17 F3	Woodstock Av. PO8	11 E3		
Wigan Cres. PO9	20 C3	Windermere Rd. PO2	25 E4	Witley Rd. PO8	10 D3	Woodstock Rd,		Yaldhurst Ct. PO9	15 F5
Wilberforce Rd. PO5	30 C3	Windmill Clo. PO8	8 C2	Wittering Rd. PO11	35 H5	Gosport. PO12	28 A5	Yapton St. PO1	6 F2
Wilby La. PO3	25 H3	Windmill Field. PO7	9 C2	Wode Clo. PO8	8 C4	Woodstock Rd,		Yarborough Rd. PO5	30 C3
*Wildmoor Walk,		Windmill Gro. PO16	16 A5	Wolverton Rd. PO9	14 C6	Havant. PO9	20 D2	Yardlea Clo. PO9	15 F2
Muscliffe Ct. PO9	15 F5	Windrush Gdns. PO7	13 E4	Wonston Ct. PO9	15 G5	Woodville Dri. PO1	30 A3	Yardley Clo. PO3	25 G4
*Wilkinson House,		Windsor Clo. PO11	35 F6	Woodbury Av. PO9	21 F5	Woodville Rd. PO9	20 B3	Yateley Clo. PO9	14 B6
Gunners Row. PO4	32 A5	Windsor La. PO5	30 C2	Woodbury Gro. PO8	10 D4	Woofferton Rd. PO6	17 F2	Yeo Ct. PO4	32 B3
Willersley Clo. PO6	18 A4	Windsor Rd,		Woodbury La. PO9	15 G1	Woolmer Ct. PO9	15 F6	Yew Tree Av. PO8	13 H1
Williams Rd. PO3	25 F4	Cosham. PO6	25 E1	Woodcot Cres. PO9	15 F5	Woolmer St. PO10	22 C2	Yew Tree Gdns. PO7	9 A2
Willis Rd,		Windsor Rd,		Woodcroft Gdns. PO8	10 D4	Woolner Av. PO6	18 D5	Yew Tree Rd. PO11	36 B5
Gosport. PO12	28 B4	Portchester. PO16	16 C5	Woodcroft La. PO8	10 D4	Woolston Rd. PO9	14 B5	Yoells Cres. PO8	10 D3
Willis Rd,		Windsor Rd,		Woodfield Av. PO6	19 H4	Wootton St. PO6	18 C6	Yoells La. PO8	10 D3
Portsmouth. PO1	6 E2	Waterlooville. PO7	12 D1	Woodfield Park Rd.		Worcester Clo. PO5	30 C2	York Pl. PO1	6 C2
Willow Clo. PO6	21 G4	Winfield Way. PO10	22 D2	PO10	23 E5	Worcester Rd. PO5	6 F4	York St. PO1	26 A6
Willow Gdns. PO10	23 E1	Wingfield St. PO1	26 A4	Woodgaston La. PO11	36 C4	Wordsworth Av. PO6	16 D2	York Ter. PO2	24 D2
Willow Tree Av. PO8	13 H1	Winifred Rd. PO7	13 F3	Woodgreen Av. PO9	21 E2	Worldham Rd. PO9	15 F5	Yorke St. PO5	30 B2
Willow Wood Rd. PO11	34 C4	Winkfield Row. PO8	11 E4			Worsley Rd. PO5	30 C3	Yves Mws. PO5	30 D4
Willowdene Clo. PO9	20 B1	Winkton Clo. PO9	21 E2	Woodhouse La. PO7	9 B5	Worsley St. PO4	31 H4		
Wilmcote Gdns. PO1	30 D1	Winscombe Av. PO8	13 H1	Woodington Clo. PO9	15 F5	Worthing Rd. PO5	30 D5	Zetland Rd. PO6	19 G6
Wilson Gro. PO5	30 D3	Winslade Rd. PO9	14 B6	Woodland St. PO1	26 C4	Worthy Ct. PO9	15 F6	Zeus La. PO7	19 H2
		Winstanley Rd. PO2	24 B6	Woodland Vw. PO8	10 D3	Wraysbury Park Dri.			
						PO10	22 D1		

ESTATE PUBLICATIONS

RED BOOKS

ALDERSHOT, CAMBERLEY
ALFRETON, BELPER, RIPLEY
ASHFORD, TENTERDEN
BANGOR, CAERNARFON
BARNSTAPLE, ILFRACOMBE
BASILDON, BILLERICAY
BASINGSTOKE, ANDOVER
BATH, BRADFORD-ON-AVON
BEDFORD
BIRMINGHAM, WOLVERHAMPTON, COVENTRY
BOURNEMOUTH, POOLE, CHRISTCHURCH
BRACKNELL
BRENTWOOD
BRIGHTON, LEWES, NEWHAVEN, SEAFORD
BRISTOL
BROMLEY (London Bromley)
BURTON-UPON-TRENT, SWADLINCOTE
BURY ST. EDMUNDS
CAMBRIDGE
CARDIFF
CARLISLE
CHELMSFORD, BRAINTREE, MALDON, WITHAM
CHESTER
CHESTERFIELD
CHICHESTER, BOGNOR REGIS
COLCHESTER, CLACTON
CORBY, KETTERING
CRAWLEY & MID SUSSEX
CREWE
DERBY, HEANOR, CASTLE DONINGTON
EASTBOURNE, BEXHILL, SEAFORD, NEWHAVEN
EDINBURGH, MUSSELBURGH, PENICUIK
EXETER, EXMOUTH
FALKIRK, GRANGEMOUTH
FAREHAM, GOSPORT
FLINTSHIRE TOWNS
FOLKESTONE, DOVER, DEAL & ROMNEY MARSH
GLASGOW, & PAISLEY
GLOUCESTER, CHELTENHAM
GRAVESEND, DARTFORD
GRAYS, THURROCK
GREAT YARMOUTH, LOWESTOFT
GRIMSBY, CLEETHORPES
GUILDFORD, WOKING
HARLOW, BISHOPS STORTFORD
HASTINGS, BEXHILL, RYE
HEREFORD
HERTFORD, HODDESDON, WARE
HIGH WYCOMBE
HUNTINGDON, ST. NEOTS
IPSWICH, FELIXSTOWE
ISLE OF MAN
ISLE OF WIGHT TOWNS
KENDAL
KIDDERMINSTER
KINGSTON-UPON-HULL
LANCASTER, MORECAMBE
LEICESTER, LOUGHBOROUGH
LINCOLN
LLANDUDNO, COLWYN BAY
LUTON, DUNSTABLE
MACCLESFIELD
MAIDSTONE
MANSFIELD, MANSFIELD WOODHOUSE
MEDWAY, GILLINGHAM
MILTON KEYNES
NEW FOREST TOWNS
NEWPORT, CHEPSTOW
NEWTOWN, WELSHPOOL
NORTHAMPTON
NORTHWICH, WINSFORD
NORWICH
NOTTINGHAM, EASTWOOD, HUCKNALL, ILKESTON
OXFORD, ABINGDON
PENZANCE, ST. IVES
PETERBOROUGH
PLYMOUTH, IVYBRIDGE, SALTASH, TORPOINT
PORTSMOUTH, HAVANT, WATERLOOVILLE
READING
REDDITCH, BROMSGROVE
REIGATE, BANSTEAD, LEATHERHEAD, DORKING

RHYL, PRESTATYN
RUGBY
ST. ALBANS, WELWYN, HATFIELD
SALISBURY, AMESBURY, WILTON
SCUNTHORPE
SEVENOAKS
SHREWSBURY
SITTINGBOURNE, FAVERSHAM, ISLE OF SHEPPEY
SLOUGH, MAIDENHEAD, WINDSOR
SOUTHAMPTON, EASTLEIGH
SOUTHEND-ON-SEA
STAFFORD
STEVENAGE, HITCHIN, LETCHWORTH
STIRLING
STOKE-ON-TRENT
STROUD, NAILSWORTH
SWANSEA, NEATH, PORT TALBOT
SWINDON, CHIPPENHAM, MARLBOROUGH
TAUNTON, BRIDGWATER
TELFORD
THANET, CANTERBURY, HERNE BAY, WHITSTABLE
TORBAY (Torquay, Paignton, Newton Abbot)
TRURO, FALMOUTH
TUNBRIDGE WELLS, TONBRIDGE, CROWBOROUGH
WARWICK, ROYAL LEAMINGTON SPA &
    STRATFORD UPON AVON
WATFORD, HEMEL HEMPSTEAD
WELLINGBOROUGH
WESTON-SUPER-MARE, CLEVEDON
WEYMOUTH, DORCHESTER
WINCHESTER, NEW ARLESFORD
WORCESTER, DROITWICH
WORTHING, LITTLEHAMPTON, ARUNDEL
WREXHAM
YORK

COUNTY RED BOOKS (Town Centre Maps)

BEDFORDSHIRE
BERKSHIRE
BUCKINGHAMSHIRE
CAMBRIDGESHIRE
CHESHIRE
CORNWALL
DERBYSHIRE
DEVON
DORSET
ESSEX
GLOUCESTERSHIRE
HAMPSHIRE
HEREFORDSHIRE
HERTFORDSHIRE
KENT
LEICESTERSHIRE & RUTLAND
LINCOLNSHIRE
NORFOLK
NORTHAMPTONSHIRE
NOTTINGHAMSHIRE
OXFORDSHIRE
SHROPSHIRE
SOMERSET
STAFFORDSHIRE
SUFFOLK
SURREY
SUSSEX (EAST)
SUSSEX (WEST)
WILTSHIRE
WORCESTERSHIRE

OTHER MAPS

KENT TO CORNWALL (1:460,000)
CHINA (1:6,000,000)
INDIA (1:3,750,000)
INDONESIA (1:4,000,000)
NEPAL (1,800,000)
SOUTH EAST ASIA (1:6,000,000)
THAILAND (1:1,600,000)

STREET PLANS

EDINBURGH TOURIST PLAN
ST. ALBANS

OFFICIAL TOURIST & LEISURE MAPS

SOUTH EAST ENGLAND (1:200,000)
KENT & EAST SUSSEX (1:150,000)
SUSSEX & SURREY (1:150,000)
SUSSEX (1:50,000)
SOUTHERN ENGLAND (1:200,000)
ISLE OF WIGHT (1:50,000)
WESSEX (1:200,000)
DORSET (1:50,000)
DEVON & CORNWALL (1:200,000)
CORNWALL (1:180,000)
DEVON (1:200,000)
DARTMOOR & SOUTH DEVON COAST (1:100,000)
EXMOOR & NORTH DEVON COAST (1:100,000)
GREATER LONDON M25 (1:80,000)
EAST ANGLIA (1:200,000)
CHILTERNS & THAMES VALLEY (1:200,000)
THE COTSWOLDS (1:110,000)
COTSWOLDS & SEVERN VALLEY (1:200,000)
WALES (1:250,000)
CYMRU (1:250,000)
THE SHIRES OF MIDDLE ENGLAND (1:250,000)
THE MID SHIRES (Staffs, Shrops, etc.) (1:200,000)
PEAK DISTRICT (1:100,000)
SNOWDONIA (1:125,000)
YORKSHIRE (1:200,000)
YORKSHIRE DALES (1:125,000)
NORTH YORKSHIRE MOORS (1:125,000)
NORTH WEST ENGLAND (1:200,000)
ISLE OF MAN (1:60,000)
NORTH PENNINES & LAKES (1:200,000)
LAKE DISTRICT (1:75,000)
BORDERS OF ENGLAND & SCOTLAND (1:200,000)
BURNS COUNTRY (1:200,000)
HEART OF SCOTLAND (1:200,000)
GREATER GLASGOW (1:150,000)
EDINBURGH & THE LOTHIANS (1:150,000)
ISLE OF ARRAN (1:63,360)
FIFE (1:100,000)
LOCH LOMOND & TROSSACHS (1:150,000)
ARGYLL THE ISLES & LOCH LOMOND (1:275,000)
PERTHSHIRE, DUNDEE & ANGUS (1:150,000)
FORT WILLIAM, BEN NEVIS, GLEN COE (1:185,000)
IONA (1:10,000) & MULL (1:115,000)
GRAMPIAN HIGHLANDS (1:185,000)
LOCH NESS & INVERNESS (1:150,000)
AVIEMORE & SPEY VALLEY (1:150,000)
SKYE & LOCHALSH (1:130,000)
ARGYLL & THE ISLES (1:200,000)
CAITHNESS & SUTHERLAND (1:185,000)
HIGHLANDS OF SCOTLAND (1:275,000)
WESTERN ISLES (1:125,000)
ORKNEY & SHETLAND (1:128,000)
ENGLAND & WALES (1:650,000)
SCOTLAND (1:500,000)
HISTORIC SCOTLAND (1:500,000)
SCOTLAND CLAN MAP (1:625,000)
BRITISH ISLES (1:1,100,000)
GREAT BRITAIN (1:1,100,000)

EUROPEAN LEISURE MAPS

EUROPE (1:3,100,000)
BENELUX (1:600,000)
FRANCE (1:1,000,000)
GERMANY (1:1,000,000)
IRELAND (1:625,000)
ITALY (1:1,000,000)
SPAIN & PORTUGAL (1,1,000,000)
CROSS CHANNEL VISITORS' MAP (1:530,000)
WORLD (1:35,000,000)
WORLD FLAT

TOWNS IN NORTHERN FRANCE STREET ATLAS
BOULOGNE SHOPPERS MAP
CALAIS SHOPPERS MAP
DIEPPE SHOPPERS MAP

ESTATE PUBLICATIONS are also
Distributors in the UK for:

INTERNATIONAL TRAVEL MAPS, Canada
HALLWAG, Switzerland
ORDNANCE SURVEY

Catalogue and prices from:
ESTATE PUBLICATIONS
Bridewell House, Tenterden, Kent. TN30 6EP.
Tel: 01580 764225   Fax: 01580 763720
www.estate-publications.co.uk